Fast, Fresh &
Spicy Vegetarian

Fast, Fresh & Spicy Vegetarian

Healthful Recipes for the Cook on the Run

Revised 2nd Edition

John Ettinger

PRIMA PUBLISHING

PRIMA PUBLISHING and colophon are registered trademarks of Prima Communications, Inc.

Interior illustrations by Neil Cavin.

Library of Congress Cataloging-in-Publication Data

Ettinger, John.
    Fast, fresh & spicy vegetarian : healthful recipes for the cook on the run / John Ettinger. –Rev. 2nd ed.
        p.   cm.
    Includes index.
    ISBN 0-7615-1623-9
    1. Vegetarian cookery. 2. Spices. I. Title.
TX837.E88 1998
641.5'636—dc21   98-22221
                                                                          CIP

98 99 00 01 02 HH 10 9 8 7 6 5 4 3 2 1
Printed in the United States of America

About the Nutritional Information
A per serving nutritional breakdown is provided for each recipe in this book. If a range is given for the amount of an ingredient, the breakdown is based on an average of the figures given. Also, figures are rounded up or down. Nutritional content may vary depending on the specific brands or types of ingredients used. "Optional" ingredients or those for which no specific amount is stated are not included in the breakdown.

How to Order
Single copies may be ordered from Prima Publishing, P.O. Box 1260BK, Rocklin, CA 95677; telephone (916) 632-4400. Quantity discounts are also available. On your letterhead, include information concerning the intended use of the books and the number of books you wish to purchase.

Visit us online at www.primapublishing.com

Contents

Introduction   1
   How to Use Fresh Herbs   7
   Pepper Chart   8

1. Sauces, Salsas, and Dressings   9
   Jalapeño and Lime Dressing   11
   Cucumber-Dill Dressing   12
   Cumin and Dill Dressing   12
   Hot Vinegar   14
   Greek Dressing   14
   Three Fresh Dressings   16
   Harissa   18
   Black Bean Salsa   18
   Jalapeño Spread   20
   Roasted Tomato and Habanero Sauce   21
   Spicy Avocado Salsa   22
   Spicy Peach Salsa   23
   Pineapple Salsa   24
   Very Fast Tomato Sauce   25
   Mexican Green Sauce   26
   Pizza Sauce   27
   Hot Pesto   28
   Spicy Enchilada Sauce   28
   Virginia's Mango Chutney   30

2. Salads   33
   Spicy Vegetable Salad   35
   Ginger-Lime Pasta Salad with Vegetables   36
   Spicy Black Bean and Pasta Salad   38
   Curried Waldorf Salad   40
   Sweet Spinach Salad   41
   Sweet & Spicy Slaw   42
   Black Bean and Pepper Salad   43

Vegetable Salad   44
Warm Pasta Salad   45
Thai Noodle Salad   46
Zucchini, Tomato, Tarragon, and White Wine Salad   48
Watercress, Gorgonzola, and Pear Salad   50
Potato-Jicama Salad   52
Bleu Cheese and Roasted Pecan Salad   54
Thai Cucumber Salad   55
Curried Apple Coleslaw   56
Green Bean Salad   57
Jicama Slaw with Cilantro Vinaigrette   58
New Mexican Bean Salad   59
Colorful Rice and Black Bean Salad   60
Black Bean Vegetable Salad   62
Cucumber and Dill Salad   63
Ziti Vegetable Salad   64
Spicy Corn Salad   65
Spicy Pasta and Chickpea Salad   66
Bean Salad with Orange Vinaigrette   68

3. Soups and Stews   69

Vegetable Broth   70
Pepperpot Soup   72
Dilled Zucchini Soup   74
Curried Vegetable Soup   75
Thai Soup   76
Curried Corn Soup   78
Cabbage Soup   79
Zucchini-Basil Soup   80
Quick Vegetable Stew   82
Red Pepper Soup   83
Spicy Corn Chowder   84
Spicy Tomato Soup   86
Gazpacho & Creamy Gazpacho   87
Cold Tomato and Roasted Pepper Soup   88
Tomato, Pepper, and Cilantro Soup   89

Cold, Spicy Cucumber Soup   90
Avocado Soup   91

4. Companion Dishes   93

Stir-Fried Red Potatoes   94
Asparagus with Ginger-Lemon Dressing   95
Hot, Spicy Rice and Raisins   96
Simple Summer Vegetables   98
Snow Peas and Red Peppers   99
Tomatoes with Parsley   100
Rice with Fruit   101
Gruyere Potatoes   102
Quick Mexican Vegetables   103
Spicy Greens and Beans   104
Spicy Green Beans   105
Rice with Cheese   106
Sweet & Hot Carrots   107
JoAnn's Potatoes with Chaat Masala   108
Snappy Garbanzos   109
Mediterranean Rice   110
Quick Spinich with Feta   111
Gingered Black Beans   112
Simple & Spicy Zucchini Fritters   113
Spanish Rice   114
Carrot and Cilantro Rice   115
Tamarind Rice   116
Teriyaki Mushrooms and Peppers   117
Vegetables with Ginger-Sesame Sauce   118
Lemon Herb Rice   120
Grilled Ginger-Lemon Vegetables   121
Spicy Potato Pancakes   122
Saucy Carrots and Green Beans   123
Green Beans in Hazelnut Butter   124
Pineapple-Curry Rice   125
Roasted Cabbage with Peanut Sauce   126
Raw Vegetables with Soy-Ginger Sauce   128

Curried Fried Rice   129
Thai Vegetable Curry   130

5. Pasta and Pizza   133

Summer Pasta   135
Lime-Curry Orzo   136
Lemon Spaghetti   138
Penne with Calamata Olives   139
Basil and Parmesan Ravioli   140
Ratatouille Pizza   142
Penne with Peppers   144
Bow-Tie Pasta with Mint   145
Linguine with Lemon and Caramelized Fennel   146
Fettuccine with Garlic and Zucchini   148
Fettuccine with Peas and Peppers   149
Quick Lemon-Ricotta Ravioli   150
Peppers Stuffed with Pasta and Cheese   152
Mushroom-Ginger Pasta   154
Sicilian Pizza   155
Roasted Tomato and Raw Vegetable Pasta   156
Spaghetti with Hot Pepper Sauce   158
Penne with Broccoli   159
Asparagus and Leek Pasta   160
Ziti with Herbs   162
Spaghetti Verdura   164
Spicy Gemelli with Radicchio, Olives, and Tomato   165
Penne with Walnuts and Basil   166
Fresh Tomato Fettuccine   168
Asian "Pesto" Pasta   169
Sweet Pepper Cannelloni   170
Hazelnut, Mascarpone, and Gorgonzola Ravioli   172

6. Main Dishes   175

Vegetable Stir-Fry with Ginger Sauce   176
Chile Pepper and Sour Cream Quesadillas   178
Sweet & Sour & Spicy   180
Vegetarian Burritos   182
Three-Pepper Chili   184

Spicy Shish Kabobs   186
Mushroom and Cilantro Tostadas   188
Caramelized Shallot, Mushroom, and Fennel Quesadillas   190
Mexican Stuffed Peppers   192
Fiery Zucchini Casserole   194
Vegetable-Pepper Casserole   195
Black Bean One-Skillet Casserole   196
Mex-Italian Frittata   197
Colorful Couscous Casserole   198
Andrew's Mushroom Ta-Rito   200
Hot & Spicy Fried Rice   201
Ginger, Daikon, and Sweet Pepper Tostadas   202
Mexican "Quiche"   204
Curried Vegetables   206
Pepper and Bean Enchiladas with Green Sauce   208
Spicy Spinich Enchiladas   210
Grilled Vegetables with Ginger Barbecue Sauce   212
Zucchini Stuffed with Herbs and Cheese   214
Four Alarm Stir-Fry   216
Black Bean and Jicama Tostadas   218
Pineapple Stir-Fried Rice   219
Fruit Curry over Rice   220
Baked Zucchini with Pepper Sauce   222
Vegetables in Raw Tomato Sauce   224
Vegetables in Spanish Rice   226
Sweet & Sour Cabbage   228

Index   229

Fast, Fresh &
Spicy Vegetarian

Introduction

There is no tofu in this book. Vegetarian is more than tofu and sprouts; it's peppers and pasta, curries and cold soups.

I confess to not being vegetarian. However, like so many others, we eat less meat, less fat, and more healthful foods. I cook almost everything from scratch—not because I'm overly ambitious but because my son Joseph has food allergies, so we forego the luxury of convenience foods or restaurant meals. This means no pizza (dairy) or other fast foods, no convenience foods (soy and corn)—not even candy (corn syrup). Before you feel sorry for him, look at the color in his cheeks and the sparkle of his blue eyes and feel the energy of a boy who eats few artificial ingredients, little fat, and literally bushels of fruit. If one apple a day truly keeps the doctor away, he is covered for thirty years or so. His diet has us all eating less fat and much more healthful foods than we did before he came into our lives.

I grew up on the straight-ahead food of the 50s and 60s, but the food had flavor. I remember my mother, all of 5'1", standing on her toes and peering into her spice rack to make selections for "a little of this and a little of that," which were the standard ingredients in her recipes, or at least that's what she'd tell you. I've never been sure whether she doesn't remember or doesn't care to tell.

We've come a long way from the heavy foods of that era. Now we want foods that are fast, fresh, and full of flavor. Toward that end, here are some thoughts on using ingredients to get the most out of this book.

Oils   When specified, use extra-virgin olive oil. I always use this premium oil when making dressings or in any dish where the flavor of the oil is important. Extra-virgin olive oil has less than 1 percent acidity and comes from the first press of the olives. Cold-press means the olives were crushed with granite stones (the only stone that will retain cold). Pure olive oil is made from a second or third pressing. For most sautéing or cooking, you can use a less expensive olive oil.

Buy your olive oil in a can if you don't use a great deal. Light and warmth can cause olive oil to spoil more quickly, so it's a good idea to store olive oils in a cool, dark place.

For other vegetable oils I use canola or sunflower oil, but often olive oil will do as well.

Vinegars   Common vinegars—wine, cider, rice, and balsamic—are used throughout this book for dressings and sauces. Red wine vinegar is best suited for sauces and marinades, white wine vinegar for herb dressings and emulsions, rice vinegar for oriental cuisine, and balsamic vinegar for sauces and dressings. A good-quality vinegar will give your foods more depth (quality is especially important with balsamic vinegar, which should be from Modena).

Herbs and Spices   A few dishes in the book call specifically for fresh ingredients, and there is no substituting dried. For example, if you substitute dried ginger for fresh, grated ginger, it will completely change the flavor of the dish. The same is true for fresh or dried cilantro (also known as coriander). There is simply no comparison. The taste of tarragon and rosemary may be lost if you substitute dried for fresh, although the difference isn't too great for making sauces.

Some herbs have such a delicate taste that they should only be added at the end of a dish, just before serving. Chervil, parsley, chives, salad burnet, summer savory, watercress, and marjoram generally suffer over high heat.

You can increase the life of fresh herbs by storing them in the refrigerator with the stems in water or wrapped with a damp paper towel, the tops covered with a plastic bag. The chart on page 7 is a general guide for matching herbs to the type of dish you are preparing.

Finding fresh garlic can sometimes be a problem. Supermarkets routinely sell garlic that has been on the shelf too long. Looks for heads with tight, papery skin and firm cloves, be they purple or white. Spring is the best time to find great garlic.

Peppers Most hot peppers can be exchanged for others in recipes, so don't be disappointed if jalapeños are the only pepper you can find (see Pepper Chart on page 8). If you are using a pepper that is hotter than the recommended one, simply use less. Whether you like your dishes hotter or milder, choose a pepper to match your taste.

Be **cautious** cooking with hot peppers. A little pepper on the finger, inadvertently rubbed into the eye (even if it happens a little later), is extremely painful and dangerous. Use gloves or wash up well after using peppers, especially the extremely hot varieties.

Beans I'm pretty satisfied most of the time using canned beans, especially black beans. If you want to use dried, soak them overnight in cold water after first picking out any stones. To quick-soak beans, cover them with water and bring to a boil.

Boil, covered, for a couple of minutes, remove from heat, and let sit for at least an hour. Drain and use fresh water for cooking.

Peeling and Roasting   A few of the recipes call for peeled tomatoes or roasted peppers. To peel and seed tomatoes, drop them into boiling water for about 15 seconds. Drain and peel them. Then cut the tomatoes in half crosswise and gently squeeze out the seeds.

To roast hot or sweet peppers, first char them under a broiler, turning frequently, until blackened. Put them in a paper bag, close tightly, and let steam for 20 minutes or so. The skin should come off quickly and easily. Jars of roasted peppers are also available in many grocery stores.

Chili and Curry Powder   A friend tried a recipe of mine once and I could tell from her expression that she didn't like it. It turned out she had used a store-brand chili powder in a dish where the quality of the chili powder meant everything. Once I supplied her with good powder her opinion of the recipe changed dramatically.

There are inferior chili and curry powders on the market, and since quality can make all the difference in some dishes, it is worth it to pay a little extra for spices which will flavor your dish properly. Especially watch out for store brands. If you have time, stop by a cookware or health food store and get a good-quality powder.

Other Ingredients   Yogurt used in these recipes is plain, non-fat or lowfat. The nutritional analysis is based on using nonfat yogurt. Kosher salt is recommended for my recipes since it has less bite than iodized salt.

Fast, Fresh & Spicy Vegetarian is about cooking for today's lifestyles. We all know the importance of "fast" in our lives, and "spicy" is a goal for an increasing number of cooks. The third element, "fresh," speaks to our wish for good health since fresh foods are without a doubt richer in vitamins and minerals.

In the media blitz over "The French Paradox," the tendency to use fresh ingredients in France has been downplayed or ignored. You may recall that it was reported in studies that the French have fewer heart problems than Americans despite a diet rich in butter and cream. The reports suggested that it may be because wine plays such a big part in the diet, since the French consume wine with most lunches and dinners. The connection is certainly valid, since so many others have reported the health value of a little wine.

Equally valid, yet given scant attention, is how likely the French are to use fresh ingredients. While Americans gulp record liters of soda pop and are hooked on processed foods, the French will generally eat fresh foods rather than microwave a dinner from the freezer.

Fresh foods *are* healthier. Your best bet for fresh foods is to celebrate the best that is available for the current season. By using what is in season you are most likely to be happy with what you create.

Finally, ignore those voices who say that vegetarians are missing something. What vegetarians miss most is the high cholesterol and saturated fat of many animal products. And of course, grains, beans, fruits, and vegetables are easier to digest than meat. Vegetarians have markedly lower rates of certain diseases, including heart disease and colon cancer. The myth of a protein deficiency is simply that—a myth. Any vegetarian concerned about protein can throw a handful of roasted nuts onto a salad or add some canned beans (more protein per dollar than any other food, but without the fat and cholesterol) to a soup. Protein is available from beans and nuts, and also from bread, rice, corn, cottage cheese, eggs, milk, pasta, potatoes, split peas, and yogurt.

Vegetables are rich in vitamins. Sweet potatoes, tomatoes, and Brussels sprouts contain vitamin C; in fact, a sweet pepper has twice as much vitamin C as an orange. For calcium, try parsley and leaf lettuce; for iron, eat peas, raisins, or spinach; to get more vitamin A, enjoy carrots, broccoli, cantaloupe, or sweet red peppers. Only vitamin B12 is difficult to gain through vegetarian cooking but it needn't be, thanks to so many grains and cereals fortified with this vitamin.

Those who talk about deficiencies for vegetarians never seem to mention the many deficiencies inherent in the meaty diets of most Americans. Vegetarian eating is good for your health.

I had a wonderful time creating these recipes. I hope you enjoy them.

How to Use Fresh Herbs

Add this herb to . . .	Salads	Dressings	Sauces	Soups	Stews	
Basil	Yes	No	Yes	Yes	No	Add to soups just before done.
Bay Leaf	No	No	Yes	Yes	Yes	Especially good in any tomato-based sauce.
Chervil	Yes	Yes	Yes	Yes	Yes	Versatile, anise-like, best in salads and soups.
Chives	Yes	Yes	Yes	No	No	A delicate onion flavor.
Cilantro	Yes	Yes	Yes	Yes	No	Be sure the flavor of cilantro complements the other ingredients.
Dill Weed	Yes	Yes	Yes	Yes	No	Gives a sweet flavor; goes well with thyme.
Garlic	No	Yes	Yes	Yes	Yes	Almost a must with oil & vinegar dressing.
Marjoram	No	Yes	Yes	Yes	Yes	Try it fresh in scrambled eggs.
Mint Leaves	Yes	Yes	Yes	No	No	Surprise flavor in salads and dressings.
Oregano	No	Yes	Yes	Yes	Yes	With oil & vinegar it makes a Greek salad.
Parsley	Yes	Yes	Yes	Yes	Yes	Use more if using milder flat-leaf.
Rosemary	No	Yes	Yes	Yes	Yes	Has the power to refresh foods—and you.
Sage	No	No	Yes	No	Yes	Strong flavor, use sparingly.
Summer Savory	Yes	Yes	Yes	Yes	Yes	Thyme-like but more peppery.
Tarragon	No	Yes	Yes	Yes	Yes	Subtle flavor goes a long way.
Thyme	No	Yes	Yes	Yes	Yes	Staple for fresh vegetables.
Watercress	Yes	Yes	Yes	No	No	Peppery, pungent, and very perishable.

Pepper Chart

Pepper Name	Heat (0 = mild; 10 = hot)	Colors/Uses
Ancho (AKA: Poblano [fresh])	3 to 6	Dried pepper is dark brown. Use in sauces.
Banana (AKA: Hungarian Yellow Wax and Sweet Banana)	0 to 3	Yellow-green, yellow and red. Use fresh, not dried, in salads, vegetable dishes, stews.
Bell (AKA: Capsicums)	0	Green, red, purple, yellow, orange. All are sweet. Use stuffed, in salads, sauces, relishes, casseroles, sautéed.
Cayenne	7	Fresh are red to dark green. Most commonly powdered spice. Use in Indian and Cajun recipes, and dressings.
Cherry	0 to 4	Usually added to condiments and relishes.
Chipotle	5	Dried, green to red. Use in sauces and seasonings.
de Arbol	8	Green or red. Almost always used dried.
Fresno (AKA: Hot Chile Pepper)	6 to 7	Yellow-green, occasionally red. Use fresh only as a seasoning.
Guajillo	5	Green or red. Use in sauces or seasonings.
Habanero	10	Green, orange. Extremely hot. Use in cooked sauces, pastes.
Italian (AKA: Cubanelle)	0	Red or green. Stuff or use as a substitute for bell peppers.
Jalapeño (AKA: Bola)	5 to 7	Black-green to red. Use in stews, soups, sauces, salsas, and pastes.
New Mexican (AKA: Anaheim)	1 to 3	Green to red. Use in soups, stews, sauces, and stuffed.
Pasilla (AKA: Chilaca [fresh])	4	Brown to black. Primarily used in sauces.
Scotch bonnet	10	Green to orange. Extremely hot. Use in sauces.
Tabasco	9	Very hot. Use as a seasoning.
Tomato	0 to 2	Sweet, red or green. Source for paprika.

1

Sauces, Salsas, and Dressings

I am puzzled when I see the vast array of bottled dressings in supermarkets. Why pay so much for something that costs so little to make, takes so little time, and tastes so much better when fresh? Homemade dressings taste so good that it will be hard to go back to bottled once you learn how easy it is to make your own.

Dressings are simply a mixture of fat and acid, usually oil and vinegar, mixed at 2:1 or 3:1. There are two basic types of dressings. The first are the vinaigrettes, a combination of fat and acid blended with herbs, spices, and other enhancements. The second type uses an emulsifier to stabilize the suspension of the fat and acid, such as an egg yolk or yogurt in creamy dressings. Oil, vinegar, and flavor: so simple and quick.

Mixing in herbs and spices is easy enough, and you can always substitute mild herbs to make use of what's on hand, or to create something different for your family or guests. One thing is certain: once you understand how easy it is to make your own dressings, how much more flavorful they are, and how much less they cost, you won't spend much time in that dressing aisle.

Salsas can also be made quickly. Homemade salsas give the cook the advantage of making them to match the dish. Bean salsas are very quick, while tomato salsas take a little longer, and really need fresh tomatoes to be at their best. A salsa is just a mixture of fresh ingredients and, when it comes to salsas, black beans are a cook's best friend. (I think black beans are a cook's best friend, period. Always keep a can on hand and you will be able to make a quick, last-minute meal or late-night snack.)

Sauces can be the busy and creative cook's salvation. Sauces can turn the everyday into something different and exciting. Curries can be added to rice, pepper sauces to tortillas, and olive oil sauces to pasta. Dressings, salsas, and sauces are included in other recipes in the book, but here are a few favorites I didn't want to leave out.

Jalapeño and Lime Dressing

PREPARATION TIME: 5 minutes

Pour this dressing over vegetables, sliced jicama, or sweet peppers. It's especially good with Mexican foods.

2   teaspoons jalapeño, seeded and minced
1/4   cup fresh lime juice
2   tablespoons vegetable oil
1/4   teaspoon salt
       Pinch of oregano

Mix all ingredients together.

Makes 1/2 cup

Each 2 tablespoon serving provides:

65	Calories	2 g	Carbohydrate
0 g	Protein	133 mg	Sodium
7 g	Fat	0 mg	Cholesterol

Cucumber-Dill Dressing

PREPARATION TIME: 10 minutes

This is good over greens and mild vegetables such as zucchini.

1	cucumber, peeled, seeded, and chopped
1/4	cup fresh dill, chopped
1	cup sour cream
2	tablespoons vinegar

Place all ingredients in a blender and process until smooth.

Makes 3 cups

Each 2 tablespoon serving provides:

19	Calories	1 g	Carbohydrate
0 g	Protein	5 mg	Sodium
2 g	Fat	3 mg	Cholesterol

Cumin and Dill Dressing

PREPARATION TIME: 5 minutes

Another good dressing for greens. When you are preparing Mexican food, add a few greens to the plate and top with this quick dressing.

3	tablespoons extra-virgin olive oil
1	tablespoon lime vinegar
1	teaspoon dried dill
$^1/_4$	teaspoon cumin
$^1/_8$	teaspoon salt

Mix all ingredients together.

Makes $^1/_4$ cup

Each 2 tablespoon serving provides:

182	Calories	1 g	Carbohydrate
0 g	Protein	135 mg	Sodium
20 g	Fat	0 mg	Cholesterol

Hot Vinegar

<small>PREPARATION TIME:</small> 5 minutes (plus 30 minutes or more marinating time)

Use this simple vinegar to put a little fire into soups, or use it in a vinaigrette.

6	tablespoons white vinegar
1/4	teaspoon salt
1	hot chile pepper (see Pepper Chart on page 8 to choose the heat level you want), seeded and cut into thin slices

Mix all ingredients and let sit for 30 minutes or longer. Discard the pepper. (Keeps about a week in the refrigerator.)

Makes 6 tablespoons

Each 1 tablespoon serving provides:

2	Calories	1 g	Carbohydrate
0 g	Protein	89 mg	Sodium
0 g	Fat	0 mg	Cholesterol

Greek Dressing

<small>PREPARATION TIME:</small> 5 minutes

A Greek-style salad is such a nice and colorful accompaniment to so many dishes, I've included this simple standard. Toss dressing with chopped, fresh vegetables, such as tomato, sweet pepper, and onion, or with almost any vegetable salad. Don't forget the feta cheese.

$^1/_2$ cup extra-virgin olive oil
$^1/_4$ cup red wine vinegar
$^1/_2$ teaspoon fresh lemon juice
$1^1/_2$ teaspoons fresh oregano or $^1/_2$ teaspoon dried
$^1/_4$ teaspoon salt
$^1/_4$ teaspoon pepper

Whisk all together.

Makes $^3/_4$ cup

Each 2 tablespoon serving provides:

160	Calories	1 g	Carbohydrate
0 g	Protein	89 mg	Sodium
18 g	Fat	0 mg	Cholesterol

Three Fresh Dressings

<small>PREPARATION TIME:</small> 5 to 10 minutes

Use these quick dressings for greens or vegetable salads. Or use vinaigrette for Yukon Gold or other small potatoes which have been cooked, sliced, and cooled.

Rosemary Vinaigrette

1/2	cup extra-virgin olive oil
1/4	cup balsamic vinegar
3	tablespoons lemon juice
1	clove garlic, minced
1/2	teaspoon fresh rosemary, chopped
1/8	teaspoon salt
1/8	teaspoon pepper

Whisk all together.

Makes 1 cup

Each 2 tablespoon serving provides:

129	Calories	2 g	Carbohydrate
0 g	Protein	35 mg	Sodium
14 g	Fat	0 mg	Cholesterol

Honey Mustard Dressing

1 tablespoon honey
1 tablespoon Dijon mustard
$1/2$ cup extra-virgin olive oil
2 tablespoons white wine vinegar
$1/4$ teaspoon salt
$1/2$ teaspoon pepper

Whisk all together.

Makes 2/3 cup

Each 2 tablespoon serving provides:

174	Calories	4 g	Carbohydrate
0 g	Protein	157 mg	Sodium
18 g	Fat	0 mg	Cholesterol

Wine Vinaigrette

$1/4$ cup white wine vinegar
$1/4$ cup dry white wine
$1/3$ cup peanut oil
$1/3$ cup extra-virgin olive oil
1 clove garlic, minced

Whisk all ingredients together.

Makes 1 1/4 cups

Each 2 tablespoon serving provides:

131	Calories	1 g	Carbohydrate
0 g	Protein	1 mg	Sodium
14 g	Fat	0 mg	Cholesterol

Harissa

PREPARATION TIME: 10 minutes

This very hot sauce is from Morocco, where it is used to spice up couscous. Try a little with rice dishes.

8   hot peppers (¹/3 to ¹/2 cup), stemmed, seeded, and chopped
1   teaspoon caraway seeds
4   cloves garlic, peeled
¹/3 cup olive oil
    Salt

Put all ingredients in a blender and puree.

Makes about ³/4 cup

Each 1 tablespoon serving provides:

57	Calories	1 g	Carbohydrate
0 g	Protein	1 mg	Sodium
6 g	Fat	0 mg	Cholesterol

Black Bean Salsa

PREPARATION TIME: 25 minutes (plus 30 minutes standing time)

A staple in my kitchen, black bean salsa in a tortilla is a meal unto itself. Or serve it alongside any Mexican foods. (If you are in a hurry, it works fine with fresh, non-roasted peppers.)

2	cups black beans, canned okay (see Introduction, page 3)
$1/4$	to $1/2$ jalapeño, roasted, peeled, and seeded
	Juice of 1 lime
$1/2$	cup jicama, chopped
$1 1/2$	tablespoons cilantro, chopped
$1/2$	red or white onion, finely chopped
$1/8$	teaspoon cumin
$1/8$	teaspoon salt
$1/4$	teaspoon pepper
1	teaspoon fresh ginger, grated (optional)

Mix all ingredients and let sit 30 minutes.

Makes 3 1/2 cups

Each $1/4$ cup serving provides:

36	Calories	7 g	Carbohydrate
2 g	Protein	148 mg	Sodium
0 g	Fat	0 mg	Cholesterol

Jalapeño Spread

PREPARATION TIME: 15 minutes (plus 20 minutes soaking time)

This fiery pepper paste works well on almost any type of vegetarian sandwich. Store the extra in a jar in the refrigerator.

4   jalapeños, seeded and coarsely chopped
1/4   cup onion, chopped
6   tablespoons vegetable oil

Pour boiling water over the peppers to cover and let sit for 15 to 20 minutes, until softened. Place in a food processor with the onion and oil and blend to make a paste.

Makes about 3/4 cup

Each 1 tablespoon serving provides:

67	Calories	2 g	Carbohydrate
0 g	Protein	1 mg	Sodium
7 g	Fat	0 mg	Cholesterol

Roasted Tomato and Habanero Sauce

PREPARATION TIME: 20 minutes (plus 90 minutes cooking time)

This is a very hot sauce. Habanero chiles should not be handled with bare hands. I put plastic sandwich bags over my hands when handling hot peppers—it's quick and convenient.

6	Roma tomatoes, halved
1	tablespoon extra-virgin olive oil
3	habanero chiles, halved and seeded
1/4	sweet onion, minced
1/4	cup water
1	teaspoon vegetable oil
1/4	cup cilantro, minced
1/8	teaspoon salt

Preheat oven to 300°. Place tomatoes in a roasting pan and rub with most of the olive oil. Bake for 1 hour, stir gently once to prevent sticking. Rub peppers with some oil and add to the tomatoes. Return to the oven for 20 to 30 minutes, stir, then bake another 10 to 15 minutes. Remove, place in a blender with the onion, water, and vegetable oil, and puree. Stir in cilantro and salt.

Makes about 2 cups

Each 1 tablespoon serving provides:

9	Calories	1 g	Carbohydrate
0 g	Protein	9 mg	Sodium
1 g	Fat	0 mg	Cholesterol

Spicy Avocado Salsa

PREPARATION TIME: 15 minutes

Wonderful with Mexican foods, and easy to make with no need to peel tomatoes or roast peppers.

2	avocados, diced
2	tomatoes, diced
2	serranos, seeded and minced
1/3	cup extra-virgin olive oil
	Juice of 2 limes
3	tablespoons fresh cilantro, chopped
1/4	teaspoon ground cumin
1/8	teaspoon salt

Combine all ingredients.

Makes 4 cups

Each 1/4 cup serving provides:

86	Calories	3 g	Carbohydrate
1 g	Protein	22 mg	Sodium
8 g	Fat	0 mg	Cholesterol

Spicy Peach Salsa

PREPARATION TIME: 15 minutes

Fruit salsas are popular in the Caribbean where they are served with many fish dishes. Try this with rice or curries.

3	large, firm, ripe peaches, diced
1	red bell pepper, seeded and finely chopped
1	sweet onion, cut in half and thinly sliced
3	tablespoons fresh cilantro, chopped
3	tablespoons fresh parsley, chopped
1/2	teaspoon jalapeño, seeded and minced
1	tablespoon honey
1	clove garlic, minced
	Juice of 3 limes
1/4	cup extra-virgin olive oil

Mix all ingredients well.

Makes 5 1/2 cups

Each 1/4 cup serving provides:

36	Calories	4 g	Carbohydrate
0 g	Protein	1 mg	Sodium
3 g	Fat	0 mg	Cholesterol

Pineapple Salsa

PREPARATION TIME: 15 minutes

This salsa is delicious alongside many rice dishes or simply for dipping.

2	cups pineapple, cut into rings
1/2	red bell pepper, seeded and diced
1/2	green bell pepper, seeded and diced
1/2	red onion, finely chopped
1/4	cup vegetable oil
2	tablespoons fresh cilantro, chopped
1	tablespoon lime juice
1	tablespoon fresh parsley, chopped
1	teaspoon red pepper flakes

Place pineapple on a lightly oiled baking sheet. Broil each side until brown, about 5 minutes each. Remove from oven and cool. Dice pineapple and mix with remaining ingredients.

Makes 4 cups

Each 1/4 cup serving provides:

57	Calories	7 g	Carbohydrate
0 g	Protein	1 mg	Sodium
4 g	Fat	0 mg	Cholesterol

Very Fast Tomato Sauce

PREPARATION TIME: 20 minutes

You can use this on pasta, cannelloni, pizza, vegetables—
whatever you need a tasty tomato sauce for. To make it spicy,
add 1/4 teaspoon red pepper flakes with the herbs.

1	small onion, thinly sliced and chopped
2	tablespoons extra-virgin olive oil
2	cloves garlic, minced
1	tablespoon dried basil
2	teaspoons dried marjoram or oregano
1/4	teaspoon salt
1/4	teaspoon pepper
1/2	cup dry red wine
1	28-ounce can chopped tomatoes (or 3 cups fresh, peeled and chopped, with juice)

Over high heat, sauté the onion in the oil for 3 minutes, until it
just begins to brown. Add the garlic, herbs and spices and stir.
Add wine and bring to a boil. Simmer until wine has evaporated. Stir in the tomatoes, reduce the heat to medium, and
cook for 7 minutes.

Makes about 2 1/2 cups

Each 1 cup serving provides:

50	Calories	5 g	Carbohydrate
1 g	Protein	190 mg	Sodium
3 g	Fat	0 mg	Cholesterol

Mexican Green Sauce

PREPARATION TIME: 25 minutes

This is a pretty typical Mexican green sauce—tomatillos, chiles, garlic, and onion are staples—and it does well with enchiladas or tacos. It can also be used on frittatas.

1	pound fresh tomatillos (about 11), husked and washed
2	to 3 fresh jalapeños, seeded
5	sprigs fresh cilantro, coarsely chopped
1	small onion, chopped
1	clove garlic, chopped or minced
6	to 7 fresh mint or epazote leaves (optional)
2	tablespoons vegetable oil
2	cups vegetable broth
1/4	teaspoon salt

Boil the tomatillos and jalapeños in salted water until just tender, about 10 minutes, then drain. (If using canned tomatillos, simply drain.) Place in a blender or food processor with the cilantro, onion, and garlic (and mint, if desired) and blend until smooth. Heat oil in a skillet over medium-high heat. Pour the sauce in and stir for 5 minutes. Add broth and salt, return to a boil, then simmer for 8 to 10 minutes, until thickened.

Makes 3 cups

Each 1/4 cup serving provides:

44	Calories	5 g	Carbohydrate
1 g	Protein	46 mg	Sodium
3 g	Fat	0 mg	Cholesterol

Pizza Sauce

PREPARATION TIME: 30 minutes

With so many focaccia and ready-to-bake pizza breads—not to mention bread machines—good bread for pizza is readily available. However, the quality of bottled and even refrigerated sauces hasn't kept up.

This quick sauce, combined with your choice of vegetables and some oregano sprinkled on top, can mean terrific homemade pizza in minutes. The sauce will keep in the freezer for 6 weeks or so, or in the refrigerator for a couple of days.

1/4	cup extra-virgin olive oil
1	small onion, finely chopped
4	cloves garlic, minced
1	28-ounce can crushed tomatoes in juice
1	tablespoon dried dill
1	tablespoon dried thyme
2	bay leaves

Place the oil, onion, and garlic in an unheated saucepan and stir to coat. Cook over moderate-low heat until garlic just begins to turn golden (but do not brown), 3 to 4 minutes. Add the tomatoes and seasonings, bring to a boil, reduce heat and simmer for 20 minutes. Discard bay leaves.

Makes 4 cups

Each 1/4 cup serving provides:

44	Calories	3 g	Carbohydrate
0 g	Protein	83 mg	Sodium
4 g	Fat	0 mg	Cholesterol

Hot Pesto

PREPARATION TIME: 10 minutes

Pesto is the easiest and one of the healthiest dishes to make—which explains its popularity. Here the pesto is spiced up with hot peppers, so you might want a cool salad on the side.

1	cup packed fresh basil leaves
2	cloves garlic, minced
2	tablespoons pine nuts or sunflower seeds
1/2	jalapeño or 1 serrano pepper, seeded and minced
2	tablespoons fresh Parmesan, grated
6	tablespoons olive oil

Place all ingredients except the oil in a blender or food processor. Add the oil slowly and puree. Toss with pasta of your choice, pour over sautéed vegetables, or add to soup.

Makes 1 cup

Each 2 tablespoon serving provides:

111	Calories	1 g	Carbohydrate
2 g	Protein	28 mg	Sodium
12 g	Fat	1 mg	Cholesterol

Spicy Enchilada Sauce

PREPARATION TIME: 35 minutes (plus 1 hour soaking and 30 minutes cooking time)

This wonderful sauce, using dried peppers, keeps in the refrigerator for a week. We use it over tortillas and cheese for lunch and dinner. For quick enchiladas, simply dip warmed tortillas in the sauce and fill with cheese, onions, and chopped chiles. Roll them up, cover with more sauce, and bake until hot and bubbly. You'll find dried chiles in the Mexican food section of many supermarkets.

7	New Mexican or other dried chiles
2	cloves garlic, minced
1	onion, chopped
3	teaspoons dried oregano
$1/2$	teaspoon red pepper flakes
1	teaspoon ground cumin
1	teaspoon jalapeño, seeded and minced
1	cup vegetable broth or water
3	tablespoons vegetable oil
2	tablespoons flour
1	6-ounce can tomato paste

Wash the chiles and cover them with boiling water. Let stand for an hour then drain. Remove seeds and stems, and place them in a blender along with the garlic, onion, spices, jalapeño, and broth and puree.

In a skillet, heat the oil and add the flour, stirring to mix. Add the puree from the blender along with the tomato paste and a cup of water. Simmer for 30 minutes or until thickened.

Makes 4 cups

Each $1/4$ cup serving provides:

66	Calories	10 g	Carbohydrate
2 g	Protein	157 mg	Sodium
3 g	Fat	0 mg	Cholesterol

Virginia's Mango Chutney

PREPARATION TIME: 40 minutes (plus 2 hours cooking time)

Virginia, my younger sister, puts up a lot of chutney each year despite her hectic schedule. Then she shares it with friends and, of course, her brother. Although this chutney takes a little longer to make than some of these other recipes, the result is worth it. This is wonderful on rice or served alongside curried dishes. It will keep for up to a year on the shelf.

2	cups sugar
2	cups brown sugar
1 1/4	cups cider vinegar
4	teaspoons mustard seed
1/2	teaspoon red pepper flakes
1	cup crystallized ginger, chopped into small pieces
4	teaspoons salt
4	cloves garlic, minced
1	cup raisins
1	cup red bell pepper, chopped
1	cup red onion, sliced
4	pounds mango, chopped into small chunks

Combine the sugars and vinegar and boil for 10 minutes. Add the remaining ingredients, bring to a boil and simmer, uncovered, for about two hours, stirring frequently, until thickened. Pour hot chutney into hot sterilized jars and seal.

Makes six 12-ounce jars

Each 1 tablespoon serving provides:

46	Calories	12 g	Carbohydrate
0 g	Protein	73 mg	Sodium
0 g	Fat	0 mg	Cholesterol

2

Salads

Salads are among the oldest recorded meals. In ancient Greece, salads were considered the foods of the gods. The Romans had exotic salads with pennyroyal (a mint), dates, truffles, and olives. They sprinkled their greens with wine.

Greeks and Romans notwithstanding, up until my twenties salads were either first courses or side dishes to pasta (nothing goes better with a hearty spaghetti sauce than a simple salad of greens with a vinaigrette).

I was twenty-something in the 70s when I moved to San Francisco and in that great city I learned that salads could be more than iceberg lettuce, supermarket tomatoes, and bottled dressing. It was there I discovered that a salad can be a great meal.

Salads of greens or beans lend themselves to the use of many spices. You might try adding a pinch of allspice or cayenne, a little mace or paprika, in dressings or atop your favorite salads. Celery, sesame, mustard, and poppy seeds are welcome additions to many salads. Tossed greens don't even have to be green anymore, with the increasing availability of radicchio and other once-exotic ingredients.

Be flexible when shopping for salad ingredients. If the ingredients you've planned on aren't that fresh, be prepared to substitute or make a salad out of what does look good. Salads, more than any other dish, are only as good as their ingredients. Select greens that are crisp and free of brown-tipped leaves. Choose cabbage and head lettuce that are heavy. If you are going to soak beans for bean salad, do so the night before, but be sure to pick out any stones. Or use the quick-soak method on page 3.

My weakness when it comes to green salads is cheese. I like to add a slice of bleu on the side or a sprinkle of Parmesan. That tendency is reflected in the Watercress, Gorgonzola, and Pear Salad (page 50).

Some of these salads are complete meals, like Spicy Black Bean and Pasta Salad (page 38), while others are best as accompaniments. As with many other recipes in this book, adjust the pepper flakes or hot peppers to suit your taste, for a hotter or milder salad.

Spicy Vegetable Salad

PREPARATION TIME: 20 minutes

The crunch of cool vegetables is offset by the spicy dressing. Good with a casserole or on its own.

$1/2$	teaspoon cumin
$1/2$	teaspoon dry mustard
$1/2$	teaspoon dried coriander
1	tablespoon vegetable oil
1	small hot pepper, seeded and minced
$1/2$	teaspoon fresh ginger, grated
$1/3$	cup yogurt
$1/3$	cup lowfat sour cream
2	tablespoons fresh dill
2	cucumbers, peeled, seeded, and sliced
1	sweet onion, chopped
2	tomatoes, sliced
3	carrots, thinly sliced

Stir the cumin, mustard, and coriander into oil that has been warmed over medium-low heat. Add the pepper, increase heat to medium, and stir for 1 minute. Remove from heat, add ginger, then mix with yogurt and sour cream. Stir in dill, toss well with vegetables.

Serves 4

Each 1 cup serving provides:

148	Calories	21 g	Carbohydrate
4 g	Protein	85 mg	Sodium
6 g	Fat	8 mg	Cholesterol

Ginger-Lime Pasta Salad with Vegetables

PREPARATION TIME: 25 minutes

This is a tangy salad that is good served at room temperature or chilled.

1	zucchini, sliced
2	cups broccoli florets
1	carrot, sliced
1	sweet pepper, red or yellow, cut into matchsticks
1	pound penne or similar pasta
1	tablespoon fresh ginger, minced
1	clove garlic, minced
1/4	cup lime juice
1/4	teaspoon pepper
1	teaspoon garam masala (or 1/4 teaspoon each cinnamon, cayenne, chili powder, mace)
1	tablespoon ground coriander
1	teaspoon dried oregano
1	teaspoon dried basil
1/2	teaspoon dried thyme
3	tablespoons extra-virgin olive oil
1/2	cup fresh cilantro, chopped

Steam or microwave the zucchini, broccoli, and carrot until lightly cooked but still crunchy. Rinse in cold water until cool. Combine in a nonaluminum bowl with the sweet pepper. Cook the pasta according to package directions, drain, and rinse with cold water. Combine the remaining ingredients, except the cilantro and olive oil, and then whisk in the oil. Pour over the vegetables, add the chopped cilantro, and toss with vegetables.

Serves 4 to 6

Each serving provides:

355	Calories	60 g	Carbohydrate
11 g	Protein	18 mg	Sodium
9 g	Fat	0 mg	Cholesterol

Spicy Black Bean and Pasta Salad

PREPARATION TIME: 20 minutes (plus 1 hour chilling time)

The very hot peppers give plenty of heat to the oil and, along with a little red pepper flakes, make this a spicy salad. Use gloves to handle the peppers—Scotch bonnet peppers are very, very hot.

1	pound thin spaghetti or vermicelli
2	tablespoons peanut oil
2	Scotch bonnet or habanero peppers, seeded, and cut into rings (use caution in handling!)
2	shallots, finely chopped
2	cloves garlic, minced
3/4	cup black beans, canned okay (see Introduction, page 3)
1/2	cup vegetable stock or water
1/8	teaspoon red pepper flakes
3	teaspoons rice vinegar

Cook pasta according to package directions. Heat oil and peppers in a small skillet until very hot, stir to blend, and remove from heat. Discard peppers and add shallots and garlic, cooking over medium-low heat for 3 to 4 minutes. Add remaining ingredients except the vinegar and cook 5 to 6 minutes longer. Remove from heat. Add vinegar, then toss with pasta, and chill 1 hour before serving.

Serves 4 as entree, 6 as side dish

Each entree serving provides:

563	Calories	101 g	Carbohydrate
19 g	Protein	181 mg	Sodium
9 g	Fat	0 mg	Cholesterol

Curried Waldorf Salad

PREPARATION TIME: 20 minutes

The original Waldorf Salad was created in New York in the late 19th century. Walnuts, now considered an integral part, were not included in the original. I've curried the idea and it makes a nice spicy salad.

2	ribs celery, sliced
3	red Delicious apples, cored and diced
$1/4$	cup raisins
$1/4$	cup scallions, chopped
$1/4$	cup toasted almonds, chopped
$1/4$	cup mayonnaise
$1/4$	cup plain yogurt
1	teaspoon good-quality curry powder
$1/4$	teaspoon fresh ginger, grated
$1/8$	teaspoon *each* cinnamon, allspice

Combine the celery, apples, raisins, scallions, and almonds in a bowl and toss. Mix the remaining ingredients and then toss well with the salad.

Serves 4

Each serving provides:

242	Calories	27 g	Carbohydrate
3 g	Protein	110 mg	Sodium
15 g	Fat	8 mg	Cholesterol

Sweet Spinach Salad

PREPARATION TIME: 15 minutes

Now you can get your kids to eat spinach—they'll love this sweet dressing.

1	bunch spinach, washed and torn
1/2	red onion, cut in half and thinly sliced
4	to 5 mushrooms, sliced
3	tablespoons vegetable oil
2	tablespoons cider vinegar
2	teaspoons brown sugar

Place the spinach, onion, and mushrooms in a bowl. Whisk together the oil, vinegar, and sugar until the sugar is melted, then pour over the salad and toss.

Serves 4

Each serving provides:

129	Calories	8 g	Carbohydrate
2 g	Protein	34 mg	Sodium
11 g	Fat	0 mg	Cholesterol

Sweet & Spicy Slaw

PREPARATION TIME: 15 minutes

This is one of my favorite dishes for guests. I take it along to potlucks or serve it with a casual dinner—the color is wonderful. The gingered dressing goes well with many Asian foods.

1	small cabbage, shredded
1	red or green bell pepper, seeded and julienned
1	teaspoon serrano, seeded and finely minced
2	tablespoons vegetable oil
2	tablespoons rice vinegar
1	teaspoon brown sugar
2	teaspoons fresh ginger, grated (do not use powdered)

Toss the cabbage and peppers in a bowl. Combine the oil, vinegar, sugar, and ginger in a separate bowl. Mix well then toss with the cabbage and peppers.

Serves 6

Each serving provides:

73	Calories	8 g	Carbohydrate
1 g	Protein	19 mg	Sodium
5 g	Fat	0 mg	Cholesterol

Black Bean and
Pepper Salad

PREPARATION TIME: 20 minutes

*Another colorful salad that blends oil and vinegar, hot spices,
and sweet peppers.*

2	cups black beans, canned okay (see Introduction, page 3)
1	small sweet onion, diced
1	stalk celery, sliced
1	serrano, seeded and minced
$1/2$	red or green bell pepper, seeded and diced
2	tablespoons fresh cilantro, chopped
1	tablespoon lemon juice
1	clove garlic, minced
$1/2$	teaspoon ground cumin
$1/2$	teaspoon ground coriander
2	teaspoons red wine vinegar
$1/4$	cup extra-virgin olive oil

Combine the beans, onion, celery, peppers, and cilantro in a
bowl. In a small bowl combine the remaining ingredients then
toss with the black bean mixture.

Serves 4

Each serving provides:

254	Calories	26 g	Carbohydrate
8 g	Protein	324 mg	Sodium
14 g	Fat	0 mg	Cholesterol

Vegetable Salad

PREPARATION TIME: 15 minutes (plus 1 hour chilling time)

Jicama is becoming more common in supermarkets. I enjoy the apple-like texture of this vegetable and its sweet and nutty flavor. Combined with cabbage and ginger, this salad has a hint of the Orient.

2	cups jicama, peeled and julienned into 2-inch pieces
1	cup cucumber, peeled, seeded, cut in half lengthwise, and thinly sliced
1/2	sweet onion, cut in half and thinly sliced
2	cups cabbage, shredded
2	tablespoons olive oil
1/3	cup balsamic vinegar
1	teaspoon fresh ginger, grated
1	tablespoon lemon juice

Combine the jicama, cucumber, onion, and cabbage in a bowl. Combine the remaining ingredients and pour over the vegetables. Refrigerate until chilled.

Serves 4

Each serving provides:

128	Calories	16 g	Carbohydrate
1 g	Protein	12 mg	Sodium
7 g	Fat	0 mg	Cholesterol

Warm Pasta Salad

PREPARATION TIME: 30 minutes

A great side salad or meal, especially when served with soup. For a colorful and filling meal make a two-salad plate: use this salad and Sweet Spinach Salad (page 41), or Sweet & Spicy Slaw (page 42).

12   ounces pasta shells
3   to 4 cherry tomatoes, cut in half
$1/2$ sweet onion, cut in half and thinly sliced
1   red or green bell pepper, seeded and thinly sliced
$1/3$ cup niçoise or calamata olives, pits removed and cut in half
1   tablespoon *each* lemon thyme or thyme, lemon zest, marjoram, basil
2   tablespoons parsley
$1/4$ cup olive oil
2   tablespoons lemon juice

Cook pasta according to package directions. Meanwhile, combine the tomatoes, onion, pepper, and olives in a bowl. In a small bowl combine the remaining ingredients then toss with the vegetables. Add cooked pasta and mix well. Serve warm or at room temperature.

Serves 4

Each serving provides:

504	Calories	67 g	Carbohydrate
11 g	Protein	240 mg	Sodium
22 g	Fat	0 mg	Cholesterol

Thai Noodle Salad

PREPARATION TIME: 25 minutes (plus 30 minutes chilling time)

This cold salad is refreshing and light. Use any thin pasta or noodle you have on hand.

1	pound Asian noodles or angel hair pasta
1	small clove garlic, minced
2	tablespoons fresh lemon juice
3	tablespoons sesame or peanut oil
1/8	teaspoon hot pepper, minced (see Pepper Chart, page 8)
1/8	teaspoon red pepper flakes
1	tablespoon chives or scallions, minced
3/4	cup coconut milk
3	tablespoons fresh mint, minced
3	tablespoons fresh basil, minced
2	tablespoons fresh ginger, grated
2	carrots, sliced
1	sweet pepper, seeded and julienned
1	cup snow peas, halved
1/2	cup water chestnuts

Cook noodles according to package directions. Mix the next 10 ingredients in a bowl and set aside. Cook carrots until just tender, retaining some crispness. Blanch the pepper and snow peas, and rinse under cold water. Combine the vegetables with the water chestnuts, add the sauce, then toss with noodles. Mix well and refrigerate until cool, about 30 minutes.

Serves 4

Each serving provides:

673	Calories	102 g	Carbohydrate
18 g	Protein	31 mg	Sodium
22 g	Fat	0 mg	Cholesterol

Zucchini, Tomato, Tarragon, and White Wine Salad

PREPARATION TIME: 20 minutes

This is wonderful in the summer with fresh tomatoes and tarragon. I recommend using fresh tarragon for best results in this recipe but if you must make it without, add half the amount of tarragon (dried) to the dressing, not to the zucchini-tomato-onion mixture.

2	zucchinis, cut in half lengthwise then cut into pieces
3	small tomatoes, cut into wedges
1	small sweet or red onion, halved and thinly sliced
1 1/2	tablespoons fresh tarragon, chopped
6	tablespoons extra-virgin olive oil
2	tablespoons tarragon or white wine vinegar
2	tablespoons dry white wine
1/3	cup extra-virgin olive oil
2	tablespoons green onion, minced
1/2	teaspoon salt
1/2	teaspoon pepper

Combine the zucchini, tomatoes, onion, and tarragon in a bowl and mix. Combine the remaining ingredients and whisk to blend, then toss with the vegetable mixture to coat.

Serves 4 to 6

Each serving provides:

260	Calories	7 g	Carbohydrate
2 g	Protein	184 mg	Sodium
26 g	Fat	0 mg	Cholesterol

Watercress, Gorgonzola, and Pear Salad

PREPARATION TIME: 15 minutes

I like to use walnut oil in salads, but it can go bad relatively fast—within a few months. When buying walnut oil, see if it is available in a can or store in a dark, cool place for longer life.

This is a delightful summer salad. Serve with Ratatouille Pizza (page 142) or grilled vegetables.

1/3	cup extra-virgin olive oil
1/4	cup walnut oil
1/4	cup balsamic vinegar
1	teaspoon lemon juice
1/8	teaspoon salt
1/4	teaspoon pepper
	Red leaf lettuce leaves
1	bunch watercress
2	Comice pears, sliced
1	Newton or Granny Smith apple, sliced
2	tablespoons broken walnuts, toasted
1/2	cup Gorgonzola cheese, crumbled

Combine the oils, vinegar, lemon juice, salt, and pepper in a bowl and whisk until blended. On each plate, place a lettuce leaf, some watercress, and a few pear and apple slices. Sprinkle with dressing; add the walnut pieces and crumbled cheese on top.

Serves 4

Each serving provides:

404	Calories	23 g	Carbohydrate
5 g	Protein	290 mg	Sodium
34 g	Fat	11 mg	Cholesterol

Potato-Jicama Salad

PREPARATION TIME: 30 minutes (plus 1 hour chilling time)

This isn't a spicy salad, and the jicama gives it a nice, fresh flavor. If you must have fire, substitute a teaspoon of minced and seeded jalapeño for the dill.

3	pounds red potatoes, whole, unpeeled
1	sweet onion, cut in half and thinly sliced
1	stalk celery, diced
1	cup jicama, peeled and diced
1/3	cup black olives, sliced
1/3	cup sweet pickle, sliced
1/2	red pepper, seeded and diced
3/4	cup nonfat sour cream
3/4	cup reduced-calorie mayonnaise
1/8	teaspoon salt
1/8	teaspoon pepper
3	teaspoons lemon juice
2	teaspoons Dijon mustard
1	teaspoon fresh dill, chopped

Cook potatoes in boiling water until soft, about 15 minutes. Remove, rinse under cold water, and cut into pieces, but do not peel. Toss with the onion, celery, jicama, olives, pickle, and pepper. Combine the remaining ingredients in a bowl and mix well, then toss with the salad and chill for at least 1 hour.

Serves 6

Each serving provides:

341	Calories	61 g	Carbohydrate
8 g	Protein	490 mg	Sodium
7 g	Fat	0 mg	Cholesterol

Bleu Cheese and
Roasted Pecan Salad

PREPARATION TIME: 20 minutes

This spicy salad is my version of one I had in a Portland restaurant. Green lettuces, not bitter greens like arugula, are best.

4	cups lettuces (such as red, butter, romaine, etc.)
1/2	Granny Smith apple, thinly sliced
1/4	cup pecans, roasted
1/4	cup bleu cheese
1/2	cup extra-virgin olive oil
1/4	cup balsamic vinegar
3	tablespoons lemon juice
1	clove garlic, minced
1/2	teaspoon hot sauce
1/8	teaspoon salt
1/8	teaspoon pepper

Place the greens on salad plates. Add the apple slices, then sprinkle pecans and cheese over each. Whisk the remaining ingredients together and sprinkle over salads.

Serves 4 to 6

Each serving provides:

246	Calories	7 g	Carbohydrate
3 g	Protein	181 mg	Sodium
24 g	Fat	7 mg	Cholesterol

Thai Cucumber Salad

PREPARATION TIME: 10 minutes (plus 1 to 2 hours marinating time)

This is another spicy and sweet salad. You can substitute fresh, hot, minced, and seeded pepper for the red pepper flakes if you wish. To make it more authentically Thai, use a dried and soaked de Arbol pepper.

1	cup white wine vinegar
1/4	cup sugar
1/2	teaspoon crushed red pepper flakes
1	cucumber, peeled, cut in half lengthwise, seeded, and thinly sliced
1/2	red onion, cut in half and thinly sliced
1/2	sweet pepper, seeded and julienned

Heat the vinegar and sugar until sugar dissolves, about 5 minutes. Remove from heat and cool. Add red pepper flakes and stir. Place the cucumber, onion, and pepper in a bowl and pour the vinegar mixture over. Marinate for 1 to 2 hours.

Serves 2

Each serving provides:

67	Calories	17 g	Carbohydrate
1 g	Protein	2 mg	Sodium
0 g	Fat	0 mg	Cholesterol

Curried Apple Coleslaw

PREPARATION TIME: 20 minutes

If you wish, substitute a good, quality curry powder for all of the spices except the fresh ginger. I like the mix of apple with curry.

2	cups green cabbage, shredded
2	cups apple, peeled and cut into slivers
1	medium carrot, shredded
1/3	cup raisins
1/8	teaspoon cayenne
1/4	teaspoon *each* cumin, cinnamon
1	teaspoon *each* ground cardamom, coriander
1/2	teaspoon turmeric
1/2	teaspoon paprika
1	teaspoon fresh ginger, grated
2	tablespoons reduced-calorie mayonnaise
2	tablespoons yogurt
2	tablespoons slivered almonds

Combine all ingredients except the almonds in a bowl. Chill, then top with almonds.

Serves 4

Each serving provides:

144	Calories	25 g	Carbohydrate
3 g	Protein	88 mg	Sodium
5 g	Fat	5 mg	Cholesterol

Green Bean Salad

PREPARATION TIME: 15 minutes

A quick and easy side to many vegetarian entrees.

1	pound green beans, trimmed and cut into 1-inch pieces
1	onion, cut in half and thinly sliced
1/4	cup extra-virgin olive oil
1/4	cup red wine vinegar
1/2	teaspoon dried oregano
1/4	teaspoon dried thyme
1/8	teaspoon salt
1/8	teaspoon pepper

Steam or boil the beans until just tender, about 5 minutes. Combine with onion. Combine remaining ingredients and mix well, then toss with the beans and onion.

Serves 4

Each serving provides:

178	Calories	14 g	Carbohydrate
3 g	Protein	70 mg	Sodium
14 g	Fat	0 mg	Cholesterol

Jicama Slaw with Cilantro Vinaigrette

PREPARATION TIME: 15 minutes

Jicama's soft flavor nicely offsets the herbs and spices here. In this salad it is matched with a natural ally, cilantro.

3	cups jicama, peeled and grated, or sliced into thin strips
2	carrots, peeled and grated, or sliced into thin strips
1	red pepper, seeded and cut into thin strips
1	small sweet onion, cut in half and thinly sliced
1	tablespoon red wine vinegar
1	tablespoon lemon juice
1/4	cup vegetable oil
1	tablespoon fresh cilantro, chopped
1/2	teaspoon Dijon mustard
1/8	teaspoon salt
1/4	teaspoon pepper

Combine the jicama, carrots, pepper, and onion in a bowl. Whisk together the remaining ingredients and mix with the jicama mixture.

Serves 4

Each serving provides:

190	Calories	16 g	Carbohydrate
2 g	Protein	100 mg	Sodium
14 g	Fat	0 mg	Cholesterol

New Mexican Bean Salad

PREPARATION TIME: 20 minutes

This simple-to-do salad is a good summer picnic dish.

1 1/2 cups cooked black beans, canned okay (see Introduction, page 3)
1 1/2 cups cooked white cannellini beans, canned okay
1 1/2 cups cooked corn kernels, fresh if possible
1 red or other sweet onion, chopped
1 sweet yellow pepper, chopped
1 to 2 jalapeños, chopped
1 teaspoon good-quality chili powder, preferably New Mexican
1 clove garlic, minced
1/4 teaspoon cumin
1/4 teaspoon Dijon mustard
1 tablespoon lime juice or wine vinegar
2 tablespoons extra-virgin olive oil
1/8 teaspoon salt
1/8 teaspoon pepper

Combine the beans, corn, onion, and peppers in a bowl. Whisk together the remaining ingredients, pour over the salad, and toss.

Serves 4 to 6

Each 1 cup serving provides:

209	Calories	34 g	Carbohydrate
10 g	Protein	369 mg	Sodium
6 g	Fat	0 mg	Cholesterol

Colorful Rice and Black Bean Salad

PREPARATION TIME: 25 minutes (plus 1 hour chilling time)

I enjoy cooking with rice. I like it simple with a little spicy or sweet pepper stirred into it, or more complicated with lots of spices and black beans, as it is in this salad.

1	cup rice
2	cups vegetable broth or water
1	tablespoon white wine vinegar
2	tablespoons extra-virgin olive oil
1/4	teaspoon good-quality chili powder
1	clove garlic, minced
1/4	teaspoon thyme
1/4	teaspoon oregano
1/2	teaspoon Dijon mustard
1	cup black beans, canned okay (see Introduction, page 3)
1	red pepper, seeded and julienned
1	green pepper, seeded and julienned
1	jalapeño, seeded and minced
2	tablespoons fresh cilantro, chopped
2	scallions, thinly sliced

Cook the rice in broth or water until done. Meanwhile, combine the vinegar, oil, chili powder, garlic, thyme, oregano, and mustard in a bowl and whisk together well. Toss cooked rice with the black beans and peppers and then with the dressing. Chill for an hour or longer, then add cilantro and scallions.

Serves 4

Each serving provides:

322	Calories	56 g	Carbohydrate
8 g	Protein	750 mg	Sodium
8 g	Fat	0 mg	Cholesterol

Black Bean Vegetable Salad

PREPARATION TIME: 15 minutes

This is a snap to make and good with many dishes but I like it best with Mexican foods.

2	cups corn, fresh or frozen
2	cups black beans, canned okay (see Introduction, page 3)
2	carrots, diced
2	tomatoes, diced
1/2	sweet pepper, seeded and diced
1	teaspoon jalapeño, seeded and minced
	Juice of 2 lemons
1	tablespoon good-quality chili powder
1/8	teaspoon salt

Cook the corn in boiling water for about 3 minutes. Drain and toss with all remaining ingredients.

Serves 4

Each serving provides:

217	Calories	46 g	Carbohydrate
11 g	Protein	574 mg	Sodium
1 g	Fat	0 mg	Cholesterol

Cucumber and Dill Salad

PREPARATION TIME: 15 minutes

This is a sweet, cool salad that goes nicely with hot and spicy dishes. As an alternative, leave out the vinegar and substitute 3/4 cup of lowfat sour cream. But use fresh dill if possible. Dried dill (use half as much) isn't as flavorful.

2   cucumbers, peeled, cut in half, and seeded
2   teaspoons sugar
1/4   cup white vinegar
1 1/2 tablespoons fresh dill, chopped

Cut the cucumber into slices and mix with the remaining ingredients. It's better slightly chilled, but tastes fine at room temperature.

Serves 4

Each serving provides:

22	Calories	6 g	Carbohydrate
0 g	Protein	2 mg	Sodium
0 g	Fat	0 mg	Cholesterol

Ziti Vegetable Salad

PREPARATION TIME: 30 minutes

If you don't like these vegetable choices, use any you have on hand. This salad really works as a complete meal.

8	ounces ziti or other pasta
4	carrots, sliced
2	cups broccoli florets
1	small zucchini, sliced
1/2	red or green bell pepper, seeded and julienned
2	teaspoons Dijon mustard
1	tablespoon red wine vinegar
1/4	cup extra-virgin olive oil
1/2	cup fresh parsley, chives, or basil, chopped
1/4	cup calamata or black olives, seeded and chopped

Cook pasta according to package directions. Microwave or steam the carrots, broccoli, zucchini, and pepper until crisp-tender. Mix together the mustard and vinegar, then slowly add the olive oil, whisking to blend thoroughly. Stir in the herbs. Toss vegetables with the pasta, then add dressing and toss well. Top with olives and serve warm or at room temperature.

Serves 4 as entree, 6 as side dish

Each entree serving provides:

421	Calories	57 g	Carbohydrate
12 g	Protein	281 mg	Sodium
17 g	Fat	0 mg	Cholesterol

Spicy Corn Salad

PREPARATION TIME: 15 minutes (plus 1 hour chilling time)

This bright dish makes a nice luncheon salad. It's at its best with fresh corn.

3	cups corn kernels, fresh or defrosted
1/2	green pepper, seeded and julienned
1/2	red pepper, seeded and julienned
1	jalapeño, seeded and minced
1/2	small red onion, cut in half and thinly sliced
2	tablespoons vegetable oil
1/4	cup wine vinegar
1	teaspoon brown sugar
1/2	teaspoon fresh oregano or 1/4 teaspoon dried
1/4	teaspoon dried thyme

Steam the corn for 2 to 3 minutes, until just tender. Combine the vegetables and mix well. Whisk together the dressing ingredients then toss with the vegetables. Chill at least 1 hour.

Serves 4

Each serving provides:

185	Calories	30 g	Carbohydrate
4 g	Protein	8 mg	Sodium
8 g	Fat	0 mg	Cholesterol

Spicy Pasta and Chickpea Salad

PREPARATION TIME: 20 minutes

Add a dash of Hot Vinegar (see page 14) or Tabasco sauce if you want to spice up the dressing even more.

10	ounces rotini, cooked according to package directions
20	ounces chickpeas (garbanzo beans), canned okay
1/4	sweet onion, thinly sliced
1	green pepper, seeded and diced
1	red pepper, seeded and diced
1/2	cup calamata olives, pitted and sliced in half
1	tablespoon fresh parsley, chopped
3	tablespoons extra-virgin olive oil
1	tablespoon wine vinegar
2	cloves garlic, minced
1	teaspoon Dijon mustard
1/2	teaspoon oregano
1/2	teaspoon red pepper flakes
1/8	teaspoon salt
1/4	teaspoon pepper

Combine the first 7 ingredients in a bowl and toss. Whisk together the remaining ingredients and toss with the pasta mix.
Serve at room temperature.

Serves 4 as entree, 6 as side dish

Each side dish serving provides:

385	Calories	58 g	Carbohydrate
11 g	Protein	628 mg	Sodium
13 g	Fat	0 mg	Cholesterol

Bean Salad with Orange Vinaigrette

PREPARATION TIME: 15 minutes

This is a nice salad with barbecued vegetables or any spring or summer dish.

1	tablespoon orange juice
1	tablespoon lemon juice
1/2	teaspoon Dijon mustard
1/4	cup extra-virgin olive oil
1/2	teaspoon fresh thyme or 1/4 teaspoon dried
1/2	teaspoon salt
1	cup red kidney beans, canned okay (see Introduction, page 3)
1	cup black beans, canned okay
1	cup garbanzo beans, canned okay
1/2	small red onion, chopped

Combine the first 6 ingredients in a bowl and mix well. Combine the beans and onion and toss. Add vinaigrette and toss. Serve at room temperature.

Serves 4

Each serving provides:

301	Calories	34 g	Carbohydrate
10 g	Protein	712 mg	Sodium
15 g	Fat	0 mg	Cholesterol

3

Soups and Stews

Soups are versatile—they can be a complete meal or a first course for dinner. And soup must be one of the oldest cooking techniques; certainly, soon after the invention of fire people began to make soups.

My favorite thing to add to vegetable soups is basil-cilantro pesto. Use about 30 good-sized basil leaves, blending them with 1/4 cup fresh cilantro, 3 to 4 cloves garlic, 2 to 3 tablespoons pine nuts or walnuts, and enough extra-virgin olive oil to make it just runny—about a cup. (If you don't have cilantro on hand use parsley or make pesto with just basil.) Spoon the pesto into the soup after it is cooked and save the rest for pasta the next day.

Hot soup is especially welcome during Oregon winters which, while usually not arctic, are very damp. That cold, wet air creeps into your bones and a nice homemade soup and bread is the perfect warmup. As you can tell from these recipes, cold soups are another favorite of mine, for warm summer evenings.

Because the recipes in this book take 30 to 35 minutes maximum to prepare, the soups here are simple to make, yet full of flavor.

Vegetable Broth

Preparation Time: 20 minutes (plus 1 hour cooking time)

Vegetable broth is an integral part of many recipes in this book so I'm offering my recipe for making your own. Homemade broth is much better than the canned version. When making broth, remember that a balance of flavors is what you are after. I recommend cutting the vegetables into large chunks for better taste. To improve the flavor, sauté the vegetables lightly before adding them to the water.

2	large onions, coarsely chopped
3	stalks celery, coarsely chopped
1	white turnip, peeled and coarsely chopped
1	whole garlic bulb, unpeeled, quartered
1	bunch parsley
10	carrots, coarsely chopped
3	cups lettuce, chopped
2	teaspoons fresh thyme or 1/2 teaspoon dried
2	teaspoons fresh marjoram or 1/2 teaspoon dried
2	teaspoons pepper
4	quarts water

Place all the vegetables and spices in a large pot and add the water. Bring to a boil then lower heat and simmer, partially covered, until the vegetables become soft (about an hour). Pour the soup through a colander, pressing the vegetables to extract their juices. Discard the solids. Pour the broth through cheesecloth or a strainer. Cool before refrigerating.

Makes about 4 quarts

Each 1 cup serving provides:

10	Calories	2 g	Carbohydrate
1 g	Protein	4 mg	Sodium
0 g	Fat	0 mg	Cholesterol

Pepperpot Soup

Preparation Time: 20 minutes (plus 25 minutes simmering time)

You might want to use 1 red pepper and 1 yellow pepper to add more color to this zesty soup.

2	onions, chopped
4	cloves garlic, chopped or minced
2	tablespoons vegetable oil
2	sweet peppers, seeded and chopped
1	fresh New Mexican pepper, seeded and chopped
2	carrots, peeled and chopped
2	stalks celery, chopped
1	tomato, chopped
1/4	teaspoon ground cayenne
1/2	teaspoon ground cloves
1	teaspoon paprika
6	cups vegetable broth
1	cup cooked rice
2	to 3 tablespoons fresh cilantro, chopped

Sauté the onion and garlic in the oil until soft, about 7 minutes. Add the peppers, carrots, and celery and sauté another 7 minutes. Add the tomato and spices and mix well for 1 to 2 minutes. Add the broth and rice and bring to a boil. Reduce heat and simmer 20 to 25 minutes. Stir in the cilantro.

Serves 4

Each serving provides:

241	Calories	39 g	Carbohydrate
5 g	Protein	60 mg	Sodium
8 g	Fat	0 mg	Cholesterol

Dilled Zucchini Soup

PREPARATION TIME: 30 minutes

This soup blends the fresh tastes of dill and zucchini together. It's good with crisp greens and a vinaigrette.

1	onion, chopped
1	tablespoon olive oil
2	cloves garlic, minced
2	medium zucchinis, sliced
2	cups vegetable broth
1	cup water
1	tablespoon fresh dill or 1 teaspoon dried
	Plain yogurt (optional)

Sauté the onion in the oil 2 to 3 minutes in a pot large enough to hold all of the ingredients, then add the garlic for another minute or so. Add the zucchini and sauté 2 to 3 minutes more. Add broth and water. Bring to a boil, reduce heat, cover, and simmer 10 minutes. Add the dill, simmer another 5 minutes. Finish with a spoonful of yogurt and sprinkle additional dill on top.

Serves 4

Each serving provides:

81	Calories	11 g	Carbohydrate
3 g	Protein	8 mg	Sodium
4 g	Fat	0 mg	Cholesterol

Curried Vegetable Soup

PREPARATION TIME: 15 minutes (plus 30 minutes simmering time)

A spicy soup which works as an entree or a first course.

1/2	onion, chopped
1	stalk celery, chopped
1	tomato, seeded and chopped
2	carrots, sliced
1	clove garlic, minced
2	tablespoons vegetable oil
1/4	teaspoon *each* cayenne, cumin
1	teaspoon *each* ground cardamom, coriander, dried ginger
1/2	teaspoon turmeric
3	cups vegetable broth
3	cups green beans, trimmed and cut into 1-inch pieces
2	tablespoons fresh parsley, minced

Sauté the onion, celery, tomato, carrots, and garlic in the oil 3 to 4 minutes. Add the spices and stir well. Add the broth, bring to a boil, then add beans and simmer for 25 minutes. Stir in the parsley.

Serves 4

Each serving provides:

148	Calories	19 g	Carbohydrate
4 g	Protein	42 mg	Sodium
8 g	Fat	0 mg	Cholesterol

Thai Soup

PREPARATION TIME: 20 minutes

This soup is very spicy, thanks to the fiery Scotch bonnet peppers. (Be sure to use extra caution handling them.) A cooler version without these peppers still has plenty of spice from the jalapeño and ginger.

6	cups vegetable broth
2	tablespoons fresh ginger, grated
1	jalapeño, seeded and cut into strips
1	Scotch bonnet pepper or habanero pepper, seeded and halved
1	pound broccoli, trimmed, peeled, and cut into small pieces
1/2	pound Chinese cabbage (bok choy), shredded
8	mushrooms, thickly sliced
3	tablespoons fresh cilantro, minced
1/4	cup scallions, thinly sliced
2	tablespoons soy sauce
1	lemon, cut into wedges

Combine the broth, ginger, and peppers in a large soup pot and bring to a boil. Add the broccoli, cabbage, and mushrooms, return to a boil then reduce heat and simmer, covered, until the broccoli is cooked but still crisp, about 7 to 8 minutes. Stir in the remaining ingredients and simmer 1 minute more. Remove lemon wedges and Scotch bonnet pepper before serving.

Serves 4

Each serving provides:

85	Calories	16 g	Carbohydrate
7 g	Protein	582 mg	Sodium
1 g	Fat	0 mg	Cholesterol

Curried Corn Soup

PREPARATION TIME: 25 minutes

Curries are a spice lover's best friend. Here, curry is put to good use with fresh corn.

1/2	small onion, chopped
1	stalk celery, chopped
1	tablespoon oil
2	cloves garlic, minced
1 1/2	tablespoons good-quality curry powder
1/8	teaspoon cayenne pepper
1/8	teaspoon ground cumin
4	cups vegetable broth
3	cups corn kernels, fresh or frozen
2	tablespoons fresh parsley, chopped

Sauté the onion and celery in oil 3 to 4 minutes. Add garlic, then stir in the spices and cook another 1 to 2 minutes. Add vegetable broth, bring to a boil, then add the corn and cook 10 minutes. Stir in parsley and serve.

Serves 4

Each serving provides:

156	Calories	29 g	Carbohydrate
5 g	Protein	22 mg	Sodium
4 g	Fat	0 mg	Cholesterol

Cabbage Soup

PREPARATION TIME: 30 minutes (plus 1 hour simmering time)

This is an easy, filling soup, made even better when topped with grated cheese. Serve with plenty of French bread.

2	onions, diced
2	tablespoons olive oil
10	mushrooms, thickly sliced
2	cloves garlic, minced
1/2	cabbage, shredded (about 1 pound, 4 to 5 cups)
2	red or new potatoes, diced
7	cups vegetable broth
1/2	teaspoon thyme
1/2	teaspoon red pepper flakes
1/4	teaspoon salt
1/4	teaspoon pepper
	Grated Swiss, Parmesan, or Gruyere cheese (optional)

In a large pot, sauté onion in oil until soft, about 7 minutes. Add the mushrooms and sauté another 7 to 8 minutes, then add garlic for another 2 minutes. Add remaining ingredients and bring to a boil. Simmer about 1 hour. If desired, remove single servings to bowls, cover with cheese, and place under broiler to melt cheese.

Serves 4

Each serving provides:

220	Calories	36 g	Carbohydrate
6 g	Protein	169 mg	Sodium
8 g	Fat	0 mg	Cholesterol

Zucchini-Basil Soup

PREPARATION TIME: 25 minutes (plus 20 minutes simmering time)

This soup is a tasty first course for pasta entrees or, with French bread, makes a complete meal. If you have it handy, pesto goes nicely with this soup.

1	onion, diced
1	carrot, sliced
1	tablespoon olive oil
1	clove garlic, minced
1	16-ounce can plum tomatoes, crushed
1	zucchini, sliced
1	potato, diced
$1/8$	teaspoon salt
$1/4$	teaspoon pepper
$1/4$	cup fresh basil, chopped
$1/4$	cup Parmesan cheese
1	tablespoon Hot Vinegar (optional, recipe on page 14)

Sauté the onion and carrot in oil until onion is soft, about 5 minutes. Add the garlic and tomatoes with their liquid and simmer gently for 10 minutes.

Add the zucchini and potato and enough water to cover, plus an inch or so, and simmer 15 to 20 minutes or until vegetables are tender. Season with salt and pepper, remove from heat, and add basil leaves and Parmesan cheese. Add a little Hot Vinegar if desired.

Serves 4

Each serving provides:

128	Calories	17 g	Carbohydrate
5 g	Protein	366 mg	Sodium
5 g	Fat	4 mg	Cholesterol

Quick Vegetable Stew

PREPARATION TIME: 30 minutes

This quick and spicy stew is a meal in itself—just serve with bread. If you wish, top it with grated Cheddar or Gruyere cheese.

2   onions, chopped
1   jalapeño, seeded and minced
2   tablespoons olive oil
1   teaspoon ground cumin
1   teaspoon dried marjoram
1   teaspoon dried coriander
2   cups fresh green beans, cut into 1-inch pieces (thaw if using frozen)
1   28-ounce can tomatoes (or 3 cups fresh, peeled, with juice)
1   zucchini or yellow squash, sliced

Sauté the onions and pepper in olive oil about 5 minutes, until onions begin to soften. Add the spices and green beans and sauté another 3 to 4 minutes. Add the tomatoes and zucchini, cover, and simmer for 15 to 20 minutes, until vegetables are tender.

Serves 4

Each serving provides:

189	Calories	28 g	Carbohydrate
5 g	Protein	349 mg	Sodium
8 g	Fat	0 mg	Cholesterol

Red Pepper Soup

PREPARATION TIME: 15 minutes (plus 30 minutes cooking time)

*This bold, red soup is spicy and smooth. Serve with a cooler
salad to offset the spiciness and the color.*

1	medium onion, diced
1	small carrot, diced
1	stalk celery, diced
1	tablespoon olive oil
4	red peppers, seeded and chopped
1	teaspoon jalapeño, seeded
	Dash of Tabasco or other hot pepper sauce
1	pound red potatoes, peeled and cut into 1/8-inch slices
2	cups vegetable broth
3	cups water
1/2	teaspoon thyme
1/4	teaspoon pepper

Sauté the onion, carrot, and celery in the olive oil until soft,
about 8 minutes. Add the remaining ingredients and bring to
a boil. Reduce heat and simmer about 30 minutes or until all
vegetables are soft. Place in a blender or food processor in
batches and puree. Reheat and serve.

Serves 4

Each serving provides:

190	Calories	37 g	Carbohydrate
4 g	Protein	35 mg	Sodium
4 g	Fat	0 mg	Cholesterol

Spicy Corn Chowder

PREPARATION TIME: 30 minutes

A filling soup, enjoy this in the early fall when local corn is at its best. Always good with salads and sandwiches, or as a first course.

1	onion, minced
$1/2$	serrano, seeded and minced
2	tablespoons vegetable oil
$1/2$	cup flour
3	cups vegetable broth
$1/4$	cup dry white wine
$1/2$	red bell pepper, seeded and minced
2	cups milk, half-and-half, or cream
1	teaspoon fresh marjoram, chopped, or 1 teaspoon dried
3	cups fresh corn kernels (or frozen and defrosted)
3	tablespoons fresh parsley, chopped
$3/4$	cup Cheddar cheese, grated

Sauté the onion and serrano in the oil until the onion is soft, about 5 minutes. Add flour and stir for about 3 minutes. Add broth and wine and continue stirring until thickened slightly.

Add the remaining ingredients except cheese, bring to a boil, and simmer 10 to 12 minutes. Remove to a blender or food processor and chop but don't completely puree, then return to saucepan and stir in the cheese.

Serves 4

Each serving provides:

409	Calories	48 g	Carbohydrate
15 g	Protein	202 mg	Sodium
19 g	Fat	38 mg	Cholesterol

Spicy Tomato Soup

PREPARATION TIME: 10 minutes (plus 1 hour chilling time)

Nice to serve with sandwiches or with a summer dinner.

2   cloves garlic, minced
1   to 2 tablespoons jalapeño, seeded and minced
5   cups tomato juice or tomatoes, peeled, seeded,
      and pureed
      Juice of 1/2 lemon
1/2   small sweet onion, finely chopped
1/3   cup fresh cilantro, chopped

Stir all ingredients together and chill for an hour or more.

Serves 4

Each serving provides:

141	Calories	35 g	Carbohydrate
6 g	Protein	1201 mg	Sodium
0 g	Fat	0 mg	Cholesterol

Gazpacho & Creamy Gazpacho

PREPARATION TIME: 20 minutes (plus 1 hour chilling time)

One key to great gazpacho is not to overprocess the vegetables. The vegetables should retain their texture and crunch. If you use a food processor, turn the machine on and off to achieve this finely chopped quality. For Creamy Gazpacho: Whisk in 1/4 cup sour cream after the soup has been chilled.

2	sweet onions
1	cucumber, peeled and seeded
2	sweet peppers, seeded
6	small, ripe tomatoes, peeled
2	cloves garlic, minced or chopped
1	jalapeño, seeded and coarsely chopped
2	cups tomato juice
1/4	cup extra-virgin olive oil
1/4	teaspoon salt
1/4	teaspoon pepper

Finely chop the onions, cucumber, sweet peppers, and 3 of the tomatoes and place in a bowl. In a blender or food processor, add the remaining ingredients and puree, then combine the chopped vegetables with the puree. Serve with sour cream if desired, or croutons.

Serves 4

Each serving of regular Gazpacho provides:

229	Calories	25 g	Carbohydrate
4 g	Protein	590 mg	Sodium
14 g	Fat	0 mg	Cholesterol

Cold Tomato and Roasted Pepper Soup

PREPARATION TIME: 15 minutes (plus 1 hour chilling time)

The taste of fresh summer tomatoes blended with roasted peppers and a little spice. Delicious!

2	fresh tomatoes, peeled (see page 4), cored, and cut in half
1	red pepper, roasted (see page 4), stemmed, and seeded
2	cloves garlic, minced
1	jalapeño, seeded and chopped
1/2	small onion, coarsely chopped
3	tablespoons extra-virgin olive oil
3	ice cubes
1	tablespoon fresh cilantro, chopped

Puree all ingredients, except the cilantro. Add 1/4 cup cold water, stir in cilantro, and chill for 1 hour.

Serves 4 as a side dish or starter

Each serving provides:

118	Calories	6 g	Carbohydrate
1 g	Protein	2 mg	Sodium
10 g	Fat	0 mg	Cholesterol

Tomato, Pepper, and Cilantro Soup

PREPARATION TIME: 25 minutes (plus 1 hour chilling time)

A perfect cold soup on a hot day.

1	carrot, peeled and chopped
1	sweet onion, chopped
2	tablespoons olive oil
4	ripe tomatoes, peeled and chopped, or 1 (28-ounce) can whole tomatoes, drained
1	teaspoon jalapeño, seeded and minced
2	New Mexican peppers, peeled, seeded, and chopped, or 1 (4-ounce) can of green chiles
2	cloves garlic, minced
5	tablespoons fresh cilantro, chopped

Sauté the carrot and onion in the oil until just softened, about 6 minutes. Add the tomatoes, peppers, and garlic, and sauté gently for 8 to 10 minutes longer. Place all in a blender or food processor along with the cilantro and puree. Chill at least 1 hour before serving.

Serves 4 as a side dish or starter

Each serving provides:

130	Calories	16 g	Carbohydrate
3 g	Protein	25 mg	Sodium
7 g	Fat	0 mg	Cholesterol

Cold, Spicy Cucumber Soup

PREPARATION TIME: 20 minutes (plus 2 hours or more chilling time)

Quick and refreshing in the summer, this is a soup you can make in the morning and it will be ready to serve that night.

4 cucumbers, peeled, seeded, and diced (about 3 1/2 cups)
1 3/4 cups vegetable broth
2 cups yogurt
1 tablespoon white wine vinegar
1/8 teaspoon Tabasco or other hot sauce
2 teaspoons fresh dill, minced
1 tablespoon chives or scallions, finely chopped
1/8 teaspoon white pepper

Place the cucumber pieces in a sieve to drain. Meanwhile, slowly add the broth to the yogurt until smooth, then add remaining ingredients and mix well. Refrigerate until chilled, at least 2 hours.

Serves 4 as a side dish or starter

Each serving provides:

93	Calories	15 g	Carbohydrate
8 g	Protein	94 mg	Sodium
1 g	Fat	2 mg	Cholesterol

Avocado Soup

PREPARATION TIME: 10 minutes (plus 30 minutes chilling time)

A summer soup that makes a beautiful presentation and takes only minutes to make.

2   ripe avocados
1   cup vegetable broth
1/2 cup nonfat sour cream
1/2 cup milk or half-and-half
     Fresh ground pepper
1/2 teaspoon ground paprika

Combine all ingredients except paprika in a blender or food processor and blend well. Chill at least 30 minutes (preferably an hour), then top each serving with a dash of paprika.

Serves 4 as a side dish or starter

Each serving provides:

203	Calories	13 g	Carbohydrate
5 g	Protein	46 mg	Sodium
16 g	Fat	4 mg	Cholesterol

Companion
Dishes

Portland, like many other cities, has a number of farmer's markets that have sprung up around the city over the past several years. These Saturday (and occasionally weekday) markets are perfect for finding the freshest product. Delighted with how wonderful everything looks and smells, I invariably buy more than I can use during the week.

We have a farmer's market downtown that opens in the late spring with Oregon's berry harvest, filling stalls with strawberries, blueberries, marionberries, and more. Later, tomatoes begin to arrive, followed by crunchy, sweet corn. This April-through-October market season also gives us plenty of mushrooms (as you would expect in this rainiest of regions), along with a continual flow of flowers, nuts, and assorted vegetables.

The side dishes here need no hard-to-find or exotic ingredients, though the recipes cover a broad part of the globe. Most can be found in neighborhood groceries. There are Asian, Mexican, and French influences. With such flavor diversity, you should have no trouble finding companions to use with entrees or salads in this book.

Stir-Fried Red Potatoes

PREPARATION TIME: 30 minutes

You might serve these spicy potatoes with a salad or two. A green salad, a bean salad, and these potatoes make for a colorful dinner plate.

3	pounds red or new potatoes, whole and unpeeled
3	teaspoons vegetable oil
1	teaspoon red pepper flakes
1	teaspoon ground cumin
	Salt and pepper to taste

Boil the unpeeled potatoes until just soft, 15 to 20 minutes. Cut into cubes. Heat the oil in a large skillet over medium heat. When hot, add the pepper flakes and cumin and stir for about a minute, then add the potatoes, salt, and pepper. Stir-fry until browned on all sides.

Serves 4

Each serving provides:

331	Calories	69 g	Carbohydrate
6 g	Protein	16 mg	Sodium
4 g	Fat	0 mg	Cholesterol

Asparagus with Ginger-Lemon Dressing

PREPARATION TIME: 10 minutes

Light lemon and ginger complement the delicate taste of asparagus. If you want a little different taste, buy very thin stalks, steam them, then fry the asparagus over medium heat in a butter and oil mixture until the tips begin to turn black.

1	teaspoon fresh ginger, grated
1	tablespoon fresh lemon juice
2	tablespoons olive oil
1	teaspoon walnut oil
1	tablespoon scallion (white part), minced
1/4	teaspoon fresh dill, minced, or 1/8 teaspoon dried
1	pound asparagus, steamed or microwaved

Place the ginger and lemon juice in a bowl. Slowly whisk in the olive and walnut oils until emuslified. Stir in the scallion and dill, then pour over cooked asparagus.

Serves 4

Each serving provides:

85	Calories	3 g	Carbohydrate
2 g	Protein	7 mg	Sodium
8 g	Fat	0 mg	Cholesterol

Hot, Spicy Rice and Raisins

Preparation Time: 25 minutes

Curried rice is a regular at my table. When I don't know what to cook, we have a quick curry (sometimes with interesting vegetable combinations, since I tend to use what's on hand when I make this). If you like, add a sliced zucchini or other vegetable to the onions and peppers after they have cooked 3 to 4 minutes. This is hot, but a milder version without the hot pepper or with less cayenne is just as delicious.

1 1/2	cups rice
2	tablespoons vegetable oil
1	teaspoon *each* ground cayenne, cumin, turmeric
1/2	teaspoon *each* ground cloves, cardamom
1	sweet red or green bell pepper, seeded and julienned
1/2	onion, chopped
1/2	teaspoon jalapeño or other hot pepper, seeded and minced
1 1/2	teaspoons fresh ginger, grated
1/2	cup raisins

Cook the rice. Heat the oil in a large skillet over medium-low heat and add the spices (exept the ginger). Mix well, then add the red or green pepper, onion, and hot pepper and continue to cook, stirring frequently, until the peppers and onion are soft, 10 to 12 minutes. Add ginger, then stir the cooked rice into the skillet, before adding the raisins. Mix well.

Serves 4

Each serving provides:

389	Calories	74 g	Carbohydrate
6 g	Protein	8 mg	Sodium
8 g	Fat	0 mg	Cholesterol

Simple Summer Vegetables

PREPARATION TIME: 20 minutes

This quick, Provençal-style vegetable dish brings out three tastes of summer, blending fresh rosemary, zucchini, and sweet onion.

2	zucchinis, sliced
1	large sweet onion, cut in half and thinly sliced
2	tablespoons olive oil
1	tablespoon fresh rosemary, chopped
1	tablespoon fresh thyme, chopped, or 1$^{1/2}$ teaspoons dried
1	clove garlic
1	cup Parmesan cheese (optional)

Sauté zucchini and onion in the olive oil until very soft, about 12 minutes. For the last minute or two of cooking, add the rosemary and thyme.

Meanwhile, cut the garlic clove in half and use it to rub the bottom of a casserole dish. Spread the zucchini and onion mix in the casserole dish. If desired, spread the Parmesan on top and broil until the cheese has melted completely.

Serves 4

Each serving provides:

87	Calories	6 g	Carbohydrate
1 g	Protein	2 mg	Sodium
7 g	Fat	0 mg	Cholesterol

Snow Peas and Red Peppers

PREPARATION TIME: 15 minutes

This side dish is quick, easy and very colorful.

1 1/2 tablespoons peanut or vegetable oil
1 onion, halved and cut into thin slices
1 red pepper, cut into matchsticks
1/2 jalapeño or other hot chile pepper, minced
1 cup snow peas
1 1/2 tablespoons fresh ginger, grated
1 clove garlic, minced
1 tablespoon fish or oyster sauce (optional)
1 1/2 tablespoons water
1 teaspoon brown sugar

Heat the oil over medium-high heat in a skillet or wok. Add the onion and peppers and stir-fry for 3 to 4 minutes. Add the snow peas and continue to cook for a minute, then add the ginger and garlic and stir-fry for another minute. Reduce heat, add remaining ingredients and mix well. Serve with or on top of rice.

Serves 4

Each serving provides:

103	Calories	12 g	Carbohydrate
2 g	Protein	5 mg	Sodium
5 g	Fat	0 mg	Cholesterol

Tomatoes with Parsley

PREPARATION TIME: 15 minutes

Here is a simple, beautiful dish that captures the fresh taste of summer tomatoes.

1	clove garlic, minced
1/3	cup extra-virgin olive oil
3	tablespoons wine vinegar
	Salt and pepper to taste
3	cups packed fresh parsley
1/2	cup Parmesan cheese
4	medium vine-ripened tomatoes, sliced

Process garlic, olive oil, vinegar, salt, and pepper in a blender or shake in a covered jar. Pour dressing over parsley. Add Parmesan cheese and mix well. Put tomato slices in glass bowl. Add parsley-cheese mixture and toss well.

Serves 4

Each serving provides:

250	Calories	10 g	Carbohydrate
6 g	Protein	221 mg	Sodium
22 g	Fat	8 mg	Cholesterol

Rice with Fruit

PREPARATION TIME: 25 minutes

This makes a nice accompaniment to spicy Asian and Indian foods or, if you are not strictly vegetarian, to fish.

1/2   cup pineapple juice
1 2/3   cups water
1   cup long-grain rice
1/2   mango, cut into chunks
3/4   cup pineapple, cut into chunks
       Dash hot sauce, or to taste

In a saucepan heat the pineapple juice and water to boiling. Add rice, stir well, then reduce heat to low and cook, covered tightly, for 17 minutes. Remove from heat and stir in remaining ingredients.

Serves 4 as a side dish

Each serving provides:

227	Calories	52 g	Carbohydrate
4 g	Protein	8 mg	Sodium
1 g	Fat	0 mg	Cholesterol

Gruyere Potatoes

Potatoes with cheese and cream may not make the lowfat list but my version of this traditional French dish is a wonderfully rich mixture of potatoes and cheese.

1	tablespoon melted butter, or oil
2	tablespoons parsley, chopped
1	cup cream
2	baking potatoes, peeled and sliced
2	cloves garlic, minced
1	cup Gruyere cheese, shredded
	Salt and pepper (optional)

Preheat oven to 350°. Brush a baking dish with the butter or oil. Mix the parsley and the cream together. Layer half of the potatoes in the dish and sprinkle with the garlic and half of the cheese. Pour half of the cream-parsley mixture over the potatoes. Repeat the process with the remaining ingredients and top with salt and pepper if desired. Bake about 1 hour or until brown.

Serves 4

Each serving provides:

366	Calories	27 g	Carbohydrate
12 g	Protein	134 mg	Sodium
24 g	Fat	79 mg	Cholesterol

Quick Mexican Vegetables

Preparation Time: 15 minutes

These go nicely with any Mexican dish, or simply serve with rice and beans.

3   tablespoons vegetable oil
1   sweet onion, thinly sliced
1   red bell pepper, seeded and julienned
1   zucchini, cut into 3-inch strips
1/2 pound jicama, cut into 3-inch strips
1   small chayote squash, halved, seeded, and cut into matchsticks
1/4 teaspoon ground cumin
1/8 teaspoon cayenne
3   tablespoons fresh cilantro, chopped
     Juice of 1/2 lime

Heat the oil in a skillet and add remaining ingredients, except cilantro and lime juice. Stir-fry until crisp-tender. Stir in fresh cilantro and sprinkle with lime juice.

Serves 6

Each serving provides:

101	Calories	9 g	Carbohydrate
1 g	Protein	4 mg	Sodium
7 g	Fat	0 mg	Cholesterol

Spicy Greens and Beans

PREPARATION TIME: 25 minutes

An unusual mixture of fresh greens and beans with the addition of spicy red pepper flakes. You might try it when serving soup as a main dish.

1	tablespoon sesame or peanut oil
1	small red or green bell pepper, chopped
1	clove garlic, minced
1	tablespoon fresh ginger, grated
1 1/2	pounds bok choy, chopped
1	cup kidney beans or black beans, canned okay (see Introduction, page 3)
1/8	teaspoon red pepper flakes
1	teaspoon soy sauce or tamari, or to taste

Heat the oil in a wok or skillet and sauté the bell pepper over medium heat for about 5 minutes. Stir in the garlic and ginger, then add bok choy and stir-fry for 2 minutes. Add beans, red pepper flakes, and soy sauce and continue to stir-fry for 4 to 5 minutes.

Serves 4

Each serving provides:

113	Calories	15 g	Carbohydrate
6 g	Protein	415 mg	Sodium
4 g	Fat	0 mg	Cholesterol

Spicy Green Beans

PREPARATION TIME: 30 minutes

The roasted peppers give an almost smoky flavor to the beans.

2   tomatoes
1   onion, chopped
1   tablespoon vegetable oil
3   jalapeños, seeded, roasted (see Introduction, page 4),
    and finely chopped
1   clove garlic, minced
1   pound green beans, trimmed and cut into 1-inch pieces

Place the tomatoes in boiling water for a few seconds, remove, and place in cold water to stop cooking. Peel and chop. Sauté the onion in the oil until soft, add the jalapeños and garlic and sauté for 2 more minutes. Meanwhile, cook the green beans in boiling water for 12 minutes, until crisp-tender, or steam for 15 to 16 minutes. Drain, then add the beans to the sauté and cook a minute longer.

Serves 4

Each serving provides:

123	Calories	20 g	Carbohydrate
4 g	Protein	12 mg	Sodium
4 g	Fat	0 mg	Cholesterol

Rice with Cheese

PREPARATION TIME: 30 minutes

This rice is a nice match for vegetable dishes and vegetable salads.

1/2 onion, chopped
1/2 cup red pepper, seeded and chopped
1 jalapeño, seeded and minced
1 clove garlic, minced
2 tablespoons vegetable oil
1 14-ounce can tomatoes, chopped, with juice
1/4 cup water
1 cup rice
2 tablespoons fresh cilantro
1/2 cup grated Parmesan cheese

Sauté the onion, peppers, and garlic in the oil over medium-low heat until soft, about 10 minutes. Add the tomatoes and their juice, the water, and the rice. Bring to a boil, cover, and reduce heat. Simmer 20 minutes or until moisture is absorbed. Stir in the cilantro and cheese.

Serves 4

Each serving provides:

318	Calories	46 g	Carbohydrate
9 g	Protein	362 mg	Sodium
11 g	Fat	0 mg	Cholesterol

Sweet & Hot Carrots

PREPARATION TIME: 15 minutes

This quick and easy side dish goes with a great many things, from rice dishes to casseroles.

1	pound carrots, peeled and sliced 1/8-inch thick
2	tablespoons extra-virgin olive oil
1	teaspoon ground cumin
1	teaspoon brown sugar
1/4	teaspoon ground cayenne
3	cloves garlic, minced
2	teaspoons fresh parsley, minced

Steam the carrots until just tender. Mix olive oil, cumin, sugar, cayenne, and garlic together in a bowl. Pour over the carrots and toss well. Add parsley and toss again.

Serves 4

Each serving provides:

108	Calories	11 g	Carbohydrate
1 g	Protein	60 mg	Sodium
7 g	Fat	0 mg	Cholesterol

JoAnn's Potatoes with Chaat Masala

PREPARATION TIME: 45 minutes

A friend makes these tasty, lowfat potatoes for breakfast or dinner. I suggest sprinkling them with chaat masala but they are great even without it.

4	potatoes, halved lengthwise and cut into 1/3-inch slices
1	tablespoon vegetable oil
1/2	teaspoon salt
1	teaspoon lemon juice
2	scallions, minced
1/2	teaspoon chaat masala, or paprika, or make a chaat masala with equal parts cinnamon, mace, cayenne, and chili powder.

Preheat oven to 450°. Combine the potatoes with the oil, using your hands, until potatoes are lightly oiled. Place in a roasting pan and roast, turning frequently, for 35 minutes. Remove from oven and sprinkle with salt, lemon juice and scallions, and toss. Sprinkle with spices and serve.

Serves 4

Each serving provides:

178	Calories	34 g	Carbohydrate
3 g	Protein	275 mg	Sodium
4 g	Fat	0 mg	Cholesterol

Snappy Garbanzos

PREPARATION TIME: 10 minutes (plus 30 minutes simmering time)

Serve this garbanzo dish with cornbread.

1	tablespoon olive oil
1	onion, chopped
2	cloves garlic, minced
2	cups garbanzo beans, canned okay (see Introduction, page 3)
1/2	teaspoon red pepper flakes
1	teaspoon dried oregano
1	28-ounce can tomatoes or 1 pound fresh, peeled and chopped, with juice
1	cup tomato juice
1/4	teaspoon salt
1/2	teaspoon pepper

In a Dutch oven, heat the oil and sauté the onion until almost soft, then add the remaining ingredients. Bring to a boil, then reduce and simmer about 30 minutes.

Serves 4

Each serving provides:

251	Calories	45 g	Carbohydrate
8 g	Protein	941 mg	Sodium
6 g	Fat	0 mg	Cholesterol

Mediterranean Rice

PREPARATION TIME: 25 minutes

Bringing together many tastes of the Mediterranean, this rice is good with a salad or on its own—and it's great reheated the next day.

1	cup rice
1	red or green bell pepper, seeded and diced
2	tablespoons olive oil
3	cloves garlic, minced
1	teaspoon thyme
1	teaspoon oregano
1/4	teaspoon red pepper flakes
1/8	teaspoon salt
1/4	teaspoon pepper
2	cups tomatoes, peeled with juice, or 1 (14-ounce) can with 1/3 cup juice
1/2	cup calamata olives, pitted and cut in half
	Crumbled feta cheese (optional)

Cook the rice in 2 1/4 cups of water until done, about 17 minutes. In a skillet, sauté the pepper in the oil for 2 to 3 minutes, then add the garlic and spices. Stir in the tomatoes with juice and olives and simmer 3 to 4 minutes. Stir in the rice and combine until mixed well. Top with cheese if desired.

Serves 4

Each serving provides:

297	Calories	46 g	Carbohydrate
5 g	Protein	396 mg	Sodium
11 g	Fat	0 mg	Cholesterol

Quick Spinach with Feta

PREPARATION TIME: 20 minutes

This easy dish goes well with potatoes. Toasted pine nuts are also a good addition.

1   sweet onion, halved and thinly sliced
1   tablespoon vegetable oil
1   tablespoon rice vinegar
1/2   teaspoon sugar
1   teaspoon fresh basil, minced, or 1/4 teaspoon dried
1   bunch fresh spinach, washed, trimmed and coarsely
        chopped
1/2   cup tomatoes, chopped
1   tablespoon feta cheese

In a skillet, sauté the onion in the oil until soft, about 5 minutes. Add the vinegar, sugar, and basil, and cook a minute over low heat. Add the spinach and cook until spinach wilts. Remove from heat. Stir in the tomatoes and top with feta.

Serves 4 as a side dish

Each serving provides:

66	Calories	7 g	Carbohydrate
2 g	Protein	53 mg	Sodium
4 g	Fat	2 mg	Cholesterol

Gingered Black Beans

Serve this spicy bean dish over rice or alongside Mexican or Asian entrees.

1	large onion, chopped
3	tablespoons olive oil
3	cloves garlic, minced
1	teaspoon jalapeño, seeded and minced
1 1/2	tablespoons fresh ginger, grated
1/4	teaspoon ground allspice
3	16-ounce cans black beans, rinsed and drained, or about 4 cups fresh, soaked overnight and drained
1/2	cup orange juice
1/4	cup water

Sauté the onion in the oil until soft, 5 to 6 minutes. Add the garlic and pepper and sauté 2 to 3 minutes, add the ginger and allspice and stir another 2 minutes. Stir in the beans, juice, and water, and cook over low heat about 15 minutes.

Serves 6

Each serving provides:

152	Calories	18 g	Carbohydrate
5 g	Protein	324 mg	Sodium
7 g	Fat	0 mg	Cholesterol

Simple & Spicy Zucchini Fritters

PREPARATION TIME: 25 minutes

This style of fritter is popular in France and throughout the Mediterranean. Try serving these with pasta dishes.

2	zucchinis, grated and pressed to remove excess liquid
2	cloves garlic, minced
1/2	teaspoon dried thyme
1/3	cup freshly grated Parmesan cheese
	Dash of Tabasco or other hot pepper sauce
1/4	cup extra-virgin olive oil

Combine all ingredients and half of the olive oil in a bowl. Shape into patties. Heat the remaining oil in a skillet and brown patties on both sides.

Serves 6

Each serving provides:

115	Calories	3 g	Carbohydrate
3 g	Protein	85 mg	Sodium
11 g	Fat	4 mg	Cholesterol

Spanish Rice

PREPARATION TIME: 20 minutes (plus 20 minutes cooking time)

Every cook who enjoys Mexican food has a favorite recipe for Spanish rice, it seems, and here is mine. It's easy to assemble and you can let it cook while you prepare the tacos or enchiladas.

1	medium onion, finely chopped
1/2	red or green bell pepper, seeded and finely chopped
1	teaspoon jalapeño, seeded and minced, or 1/2 teaspoon ground cayenne
2	tablespoons extra-virgin olive oil
2	cloves garlic, minced
1	cup long-grain rice
2	cups vegetable broth or water
1	cup tomato sauce
1/2	teaspoon ground cumin

Sauté the onion and peppers in the oil until onion is soft, about 5 minutes. Add garlic and mix well. Stir in the rice, stirring for 4 to 5 minutes over medium heat. Add the remaining ingredients, bring to a boil, then simmer, covered, for 20 minutes or until liquid is absorbed.

Serves 4

Each serving provides:

288	Calories	50 g	Carbohydrate
5 g	Protein	372 mg	Sodium
7 g	Fat	0 mg	Cholesterol

Carrot and Cilantro Rice

PREPARATION TIME: 20 minutes

Here's a quick side dish to give rice both color and crunch.

1 1/2   cups rice
3 1/4   cups vegetable broth or water
1 1/2   cups raw carrot, grated
1/2   cup green onions, finely chopped
1/2   teaspoon cumin
1/8   teaspoon cayenne
2   tablespoons fresh cilantro, finely chopped

Cook rice in the vegetable broth or water for about 17 minutes, or until all of the liquid is absorbed. Stir all ingredients into the rice.

Serves 4

Each serving provides:

288	Calories	63 g	Carbohydrate
6 g	Protein	24 mg	Sodium
1 g	Fat	0 mg	Cholesterol

Tamarind Rice

PREPARATION TIME: 15 minutes (plus 17 minutes cooking time)

Tamarind has a rich flavor and there really isn't any substitute. The paste lasts a long time in the refrigerator and is available at many Asian markets, upscale supermarkets, and specialty food shops.

1	tablespoon butter
1 1/2	cups white long-grain rice
1/2	cup onion, minced
1	teaspoon ground cinnamon
2	tablespoons tamarind paste
1	teaspoon salt
1 3/4	cups water or 1 cup water and 3/4 cup vegetable broth
1/4	cup raisins

Melt the butter in a skillet and sauté the rice and onion for about 5 minutes. Stir in the cinnamon, tamarind paste, salt, and a little of the water or broth. Be sure to mix well but don't worry about getting the paste entirely dissolved. Add the rest of the liquid and bring to a boil. Cover and cook over low heat for 17 minutes. Stir in raisins and serve.

Serves 4

Each serving provides:

336	Calories	69 g	Carbohydrate
6 g	Protein	870 mg	Sodium
4 g	Fat	8 mg	Cholesterol

Teriyaki Mushrooms and Peppers

PREPARATION TIME: 20 minutes

Delicious, of course, with Asian dishes but also good as an entree over a bed of rice.

1	pound cremini, shiitake, or button mushrooms, quartered
1	red or green bell pepper, cut into squares
	Sesame oil
5	tablespoons soy sauce
2	tablespoons sugar
1 1/2	tablespoons fresh ginger, minced
1 1/2	tablespoons rice wine or rice wine vinegar

Thread the mushrooms and peppers onto skewers and brush lightly with sesame oil. Grill over a charcoal fire or broil in a baking dish 4 to 5 minutes, turning frequently. Combine remaining ingredients in a saucepan and stir to dissolve sugar. Heat to boiling, remove from heat, and transfer to a serving bowl. Spoon a little sauce over skewers and serve the remainder for dipping.

Serves 4

Each serving provides:

96	Calories	15 g	Carbohydrate
4 g	Protein	1305 mg	Sodium
3 g	Fat	0 mg	Cholesterol

Vegetables with Ginger-Sesame Sauce

PREPARATION TIME: 30 minutes

Try this with Asian dishes or grilled vegetables.

2	tablespoons sesame seeds
1	tablespoon butter
1	tablespoon plus 1 teaspoon peanut oil
1	onion, halved and thinly sliced
1	red pepper, cut into matchsticks
3	carrots, cut into matchsticks
2	zucchinis, trimmed, quartered, and cut into matchsticks
1/4	cup soy sauce
1/4	cup dry sherry
1/4	cup vegetable broth or water
1	tablespoon plus 1 teaspoon freshly grated ginger
1	tablespoon cornstarch
1	tablespoon sesame oil

Toast the seeds in a dry skillet over medium heat, stirring constantly for 3 to 5 minutes, or until they begin to release their fragrance. Remove from the skillet and set aside. Heat the butter and 1 tablespoon of the peanut oil in the skillet and sauté the onion, pepper, and carrots over medium heat for 6 to 8 minutes. Add the zucchini and sauté another 3 minutes. In a small bowl, combine the remaining peanut oil with the rest of the ingredients and whisk together well. Remove the vegetables from the skillet and increase heat to high. Add the sauce and whisk over high heat for 30 seconds, or until slightly thickened. Remove and stir in toasted sesame seeds. Serve alongside or pour over vegetables.

Serves 4 as a side dish

Each serving provides:

201	Calories	16 g	Carbohydrate
3 g	Protein	142 mg	Sodium
13 g	Fat	8 mg	Cholesterol

Lemon Herb Rice

Preparation Time: 20 minutes

Fresh herbs are best in this dish. A fine accompaniment to vegetable dishes.

1	cup rice
2 1/4	cups vegetable broth or water
2	teaspoons *each* fresh thyme, oregano, tarragon, and chives or 1 teaspoon *each* dried
1	tablespoon fresh lemon juice
2	teaspoons white wine vinegar

Cook the rice in the liquid about 20 minutes, or until all liquid is absorbed. Meanwhile, mince the herbs. Combine the herbs, lemon juice, and vinegar with the rice and serve.

Serves 4

Each serving provides:

178	Calories	39 g	Carbohydrate
4 g	Protein	5 mg	Sodium
0 g	Fat	0 mg	Cholesterol

Grilled Ginger-Lemon Vegetables

PREPARATION TIME: 20 minutes

I think leeks make the best grilled vegetables. They just melt and brown on the grill, giving a terrific flavor that is complemented by this marinade.

3	tablespoons lemon juice
2	tablespoons fresh ginger, grated
1	tablespoon honey
2	tablespoons peanut oil
1/4	teaspoon salt
2	leeks, white parts only, cut in half lengthwise and trimmed
2	zucchinis, trimmed and sliced lengthwise
1	tomato, cut into chunks

Combine the lemon juice, ginger, honey, oil, and salt in a bowl and whisk together. Place the vegetables in a large bowl and toss with the marinade. Refrigerate for one hour, then grill over medium-hot coals, or on a stovetop grill, to taste.

Serves 4 as a side dish

Each serving provides:

137	Calories	18 g	Carbohydrate
2 g	Protein	151 mg	Sodium
7 g	Fat	0 mg	Cholesterol

Spicy Potato Pancakes

PREPARATION TIME: 25 minutes

My mother used to make potato pancakes for breakfast out of last night's leftover mashed potatoes. I've come up with this recipe for spicy and quick fresh pancakes, but I'm not sure they're ever as good as hers—or the memory of hers.

2	eggs
1	pound potatoes, peeled and grated (about 2 cups)
1/2	teaspoon salt
1/8	teaspoon pepper
1	teaspoon red pepper flakes
2	tablespoons flour
1/2	small onion, grated (about 1/3 cup)
1	tablespoon cream or milk
	Vegetable oil

Beat the eggs and mix with the potatoes, then mix with the remaining ingredients except the oil, until well combined. Heat enough oil in a skillet to cover the bottom of the pan. Add 3 tablespoons or so of batter and spread into a thin pancake. Fry until brown, 2 to 3 minutes per side.

Serves 4

Each serving provides:

216	Calories	25 g	Carbohydrate
6 g	Protein	305 mg	Sodium
11 g	Fat	110 mg	Cholesterol

Saucy Carrots and Green Beans

PREPARATION TIME: 15 minutes

When you are serving something complicated, this simple dish of fresh herbs and easy flavors is very nice on the side.

3	carrots, peeled and julienned
2	cups green beans, trimmed and cut into 1-inch pieces
1	tablespoon Dijon mustard
1	teaspoon tarragon vinegar
3	tablespoons fresh parsley, finely chopped
1	teaspoon fresh tarragon, or 1/2 teaspoon dried
3	tablespoons extra-virgin olive oil
1/2	teaspoon lemon juice

Steam the vegetables until crisp-tender and toss together. Mix the mustard, vinegar, parsley, and tarragon in a bowl. Slowly add the olive oil, whisking it in to mix. Add lemon juice, whisk thoroughly, then pour over vegetables.

Serves 4

Each serving provides:

143	Calories	11 g	Carbohydrate
2 g	Protein	130 mg	Sodium
11 g	Fat	0 mg	Cholesterol

Green Beans in Hazelnut Butter

The Northwest has an abundance of hazelnuts and I enjoy adding them to many dishes. This may not win the low-cholesterol award but the combination of the crisp-tender fresh beans, butter, and nuts is heavenly.

1	pound green beans, trimmed
3	tablespoons unsalted butter
1/3	cup hazelnuts, skinned and chopped

Cook the beans in boiling water until just tender, about 3 minutes. Drain and place in a pot of cold water to stop the cooking process. Melt the butter in a large skillet and add the beans. Stir-fry for 2 minutes, then add the hazelnuts and stir to combine well. Remove from heat and serve.

Serves 4

Each serving provides:

183	Calories	11 g	Carbohydrate
3 g	Protein	5 mg	Sodium
16 g	Fat	25 mg	Cholesterol

Pineapple-Curry Rice

PREPARATION TIME: 20 minutes

This sweet and spicy dish is a little too intense as a dish on its own. Serve with shish kabobs or a stir-fry.

1/4	teaspoon *each* cardamom, turmeric, ground coriander, cumin, cayenne
1/8	teaspoon *each* ground cloves, nutmeg
1/2	teaspoon sweet paprika
2	cloves garlic, minced
1 1/2	teaspoons fresh ginger, grated
1	tablespoon brown sugar
1/4	cup pineapple juice
1/2	cup pineapple, finely diced
	Cooked rice

Stir the spices together in a small skillet on low heat for a minute or two. Add the garlic, ginger, sugar, and pineapple juice, and cook on medium heat, stirring frequently, for 5 to 7 minutes. Remove from heat and add the pineapple. Serve on the side with the rice.

Serves 4

Each serving not including rice provides:

55	Calories	14 g	Carbohydrate
0 g	Protein	4 mg	Sodium
0 g	Fat	0 mg	Cholesterol

Roasted Cabbage with Peanut Sauce

PREPARATION TIME: 35 minutes

Roasted cabbage is wonderful on its own, but I think it's even better with this peanut sauce. You can use this sauce over other cooked vegetables as well.

1	head green cabbage, sliced
3	tablespoons melted butter or olive oil
1/2	cup peanut butter
	Dash of hot sauce
3	tablespoons fresh ginger, grated
2	teaspoons garlic, minced
2	tablespoons soy or tamari sauce
1	teaspoon rice vinegar
1	teaspoon honey
1/8	teaspoon salt
	Pinch of cayenne
1/2	cup water

Preheat oven to 500°. Toss the cabbage with the butter or oil (don't worry about coating each and every piece). Bake for 12 to 15 minutes, then toss the pieces. Bake for another 12 to 15 minutes, until cabbage just begins to brown.

Combine the remaining ingredients in a blender and process until smooth, using additional water if necessary. Serve alongside or pour over the cabbage.

Serves 4 as a side dish

Each serving provides:

332	Calories	22 g	Carbohydrate
11 g	Protein	867 mg	Sodium
26 g	Fat	25 mg	Cholesterol

Raw Vegetables with Soy-Ginger Sauce

Raw vegetables covered with a sauce go nicely with many Asian dishes. Use the seasonal, fresh vegetables you have on hand.

1/4   cup tamari or soy sauce
1/4   cup water
1   teaspoon sherry
1 1/2 tablespoons fresh ginger, grated
1   teaspoon vegetable oil
1/2   teaspoon sugar
3   carrots, peeled and cut into sticks
1   head broccoli or cauliflower florets
6   button mushrooms

Whisk the tamari or soy sauce, water, sherry, ginger, oil, and sugar together; let stand for 30 minutes. Meanwhile, slice or chop the vegetables, and toss together. Strain to remove ginger strings from sauce and pour over raw vegetables.

Serves 4

Each serving provides:

80	Calories	13 g	Carbohydrate
5 g	Protein	1057 mg	Sodium
2 g	Fat	0 mg	Cholesterol

Curried Fried Rice

PREPARATION TIME: 15 minutes

Fried rice works best when the rice is cold so this is an ideal dish for using last night's rice. It's an excuse for making too much rice tonight so you can have curried fried rice tomorrow! Be sure to separate the cold rice with a fork before stirring in.

5 tablespoons vegetable broth or water
1 tablespoon soy sauce
1 teaspoon fresh ginger, grated
1/2 teaspoon salt
2 tablespoons vegetable oil
1 small onion, finely chopped
2 carrots, peeled and finely chopped
2 tablespoons good-quality curry powder
1 cup fresh peas steamed 2 to 3 minutes, or frozen peas, thawed
3 1/2 cups cold, cooked rice

Combine the first 4 ingredients in a bowl and set aside. Heat the oil in a wok or skillet over medium-high, add the onion and carrot and stir-fry 3 to 4 minutes. Add the curry powder, stir in well, then add the peas and stir-fry just until heated, about a minute or two. Add rice, stir in well to mix, then add sauce. Remove from heat and toss to mix well.

Serves 4

Each serving provides:

367	Calories	65 g	Carbohydrate
8 g	Protein	581 mg	Sodium
8 g	Fat	0 mg	Cholesterol

Thai Vegetable Curry

PREPARATION TIME: 25 minutes

If you don't have one of these vegetables, substitute a carrot, chayote squash, sweet potato, peas, or other vegetable. Many vegetables will work in this dish. If you don't have the curry paste you can omit it, but be sure to cut the broth or water in half if you do.

1	zucchini, sliced about 1/4-inch thick
1 1/2	cups cauliflower, sliced about 1/4-inch thick
1	cup green beans, trimmed and sliced
1	potato
1	red pepper, cut into matchsticks
1	tablespoon vegetable oil
1	clove garlic, minced
1 1/2	teaspoons red curry paste
1	tablespoon freshly minced ginger
1	tablespoon good-quality curry powder
1	teaspoon ground cumin
2	teaspoons ground coriander
2	cups light coconut milk
1	cup vegetable broth or water
2	tablespoons brown sugar
1	tablespoon soy sauce
2	tablespoons cilantro, chopped

Blanch the zucchini, cauliflower, and beans in boiling water for 2 to 3 minutes, then rinse in cold water. Microwave the potato until just tender, cool, and cut into cubes. Combine the vegetables in a bowl (including the pepper) and set aside. Heat the oil in a skillet and add the garlic, curry paste, ginger, curry powder, cumin, and coriander and sauté, stirring constantly over low heat, for a minute or so to release flavors. Add the coconut milk, broth or water, brown sugar, and soy sauce and bring to a simmer. Add the vegetables and reduce the heat. Cook until heated throughout. Remove from heat and add cilantro.

Serves 4

Each serving provides:

223	Calories	30 g	Carbohydrate
4 g	Protein	454 mg	Sodium
11 g	Fat	0 mg	Cholesterol

5

Pasta and Pizza

Among the new recipes in this revised edition of *Fast, Fresh & Spicy Vegetarian* are three quick ravioli recipes. Few things are as fun to invent—and to eat—as ravioli. Making the pasta is the time-consuming part, since the filling is simply a mixture of just two or three ingredients.

Over the past few years, there has been a much greater interest in fresh pasta and, as a result, many more places to buy fresh pasta. In Portland, where I live, I've discovered a little shop called Justa Pasta. Located in an industrial district close to downtown, it's a great place to pick up fresh ravioli or lasagna sheets to make my own dishes. To me, two dollars for homemade pasta is the best food bargain in town. Justa Pasta isn't the only place to buy pasta. In Portland there are a half-dozen other stores where I could buy sheets.

That's why I've included quick ravioli recipes in this section. If there is so much fresh pasta available in Portland, you can probably find fresh pasta where you live. Look in the phone book under pasta, call upscale supermarkets, or check the packages of fresh pasta sold in stores for the name of the maker. If you simply can't get fresh pasta, try wonton wrappers, which are usually available in the supermarket freezer section.

One simple ravioli or pasta taste-enhancer is to flavor your olive oil. For example, a sprig of fresh rosemary added to oil over low heat for 20 or 30 minutes will infuse the oil with the flavor of that herb. The rosemary-infused oil nicely complements pasta tossed with fresh vegetables, or it may be drizzled over ravioli. The same is true for other ingredients including peppers, which can infuse the oil with heat, as they do in the Spaghetti with Hot Pepper Sauce (page 158). Peppers can also add flavor to the water you use to cook the pasta, and thereby add flavor to the pasta. The very spicy Scotch bonnet peppers are used for that purpose in the Ziti with Herbs recipe (page 162).

Serving a cheese bread or bread rubbed with oil and garlic goes well with many pasta dishes, of course. For cheese bread, I just slice a baguette, rub the slices with butter or oil, rub them again with minced garlic, sprinkle on fresh Parmesan, then broil them briefly to melt the cheese.

For the spicier pastas you may want to add a few slices of cold carrot or cucumber on the plate to refresh the palate. If the heat of a dish is too much for the kids, consider recipes where you can add the spice toward the end, and make two versions, one hot and one mild. Also remember, fresh herbs and spices can usually be added later than dried ones.

In the "Sauces, Salsas, and Dressings" chapter you can find a recipe for pizza sauce (page 27) that may be added to any pizzas. Just cover the crust with the pizza sauce after you use the olive oil, then add the toppings of your choice.

Summer Pasta

PREPARATION TIME: 20 minutes

This colorful pasta is a snap to make. Be sure not to overpower the asparagus with too much heat in the sauce or with the jalapeño peppers.

1   pound angel hair pasta
3/4   pound asparagus, trimmed and cut into 1-inch lengths
1   tablespoon extra-virgin olive oil
1 1/2   cups roasted red or yellow sweet pepper, cut into match-
        sticks or squares
1/2   jalapeño pepper, seeded and minced (do not use if
        peppers were added to the Very Fast Tomato Sauce)
2 1/2   cups Very Fast Tomato Sauce (page 25) or tomato sauce
        of your choice
1   clove garlic, minced

Cook the pasta according to package instructions and drain. Steam, boil, or microwave the asparagus until just crisp-tender. Heat the oil in a skillet and sauté the peppers until crisp-tender, about 6 minutes. Heat the sauce, stirring in the garlic. Toss the pasta with the vegetables, then top with the tomato sauce.

Serves 4

Each 1 cup serving provides:

622	Calories	107 g	Carbohydrate
19 g	Protein	696 mg	Sodium
13 g	Fat	0 mg	Cholesterol

Lime-Curry Orzo

PREPARATION TIME: 25 minutes

I like to have a simple, green salad with this somewhat unusual pasta dish.

8	ounces orzo or other small pasta
4	tablespoons vegetable oil
1/3	cup onion, minced
1	stalk celery, thinly sliced
1/4	teaspoon *each* turmeric, ground coriander, cardamom, and sweet paprika
1/8	teaspoon *each* ground cumin, cloves, and cayenne
2	tablespoons fresh ginger, grated
1	teaspoon salt
1/2	teaspoon pepper
2	tablespoons lime juice
12	calamata or black olives
1/2	cup crumbled feta cheese (optional)

Cook the orzo according to package directions. In 1 tablespoon of the oil, sauté the onion over low heat for 5 minutes or until soft, adding the celery for the last few minutes. Add the spices except the ginger, salt, and pepper, mixing well. Remove from heat and stir in the ginger, salt, pepper, lime juice, olives, and remaining 3 tablespoons of oil. Top with the cheese if desired.

Serves 4

Each serving provides:

361	Calories	46 g	Carbohydrate
8 g	Protein	659 mg	Sodium
16 g	Fat	0 mg	Cholesterol

Lemon Spaghetti

PREPARATION TIME: 20 minutes

This is a simple pasta to serve at the end of a busy day, and easy to make since it calls for ingredients you are likely to have on hand. Garlic bread or focaccia goes well with it.

1	pound spaghetti
1	tablespoon olive oil
3	zucchinis, sliced
2	tablespoons fresh basil, chopped, or 2 teaspoons dried
7	mushrooms, sliced
3	to 4 cloves garlic, minced
	Juice of 1 1/2 lemons
1	cup fresh Parmesan or pecorino cheese, grated (optional)

Cook pasta according to package directions. Heat the olive oil in a skillet and add the zucchini and basil. Cook over medium heat for about 5 minutes, then add mushrooms and cook another 5 minutes. Add garlic, stir, and cook for 2 minutes, then pour in the lemon juice and remove from heat. Toss with the cooked and drained pasta; top with the cheese if desired.

Serves 4

Each serving provides:

504	Calories	96 g	Carbohydrate
17 g	Protein	9 mg	Sodium
6 g	Fat	0 mg	Cholesterol

Penne with Calamata Olives

PREPARATION TIME: 20 minutes

The fresh taste of the spices together with the strong olives gives this dish a nice Mediterranean taste. If you're feeling Italian, use the Parmesan; if it's Greek, use feta!

1	pound penne
1/2	onion, minced
1	tablespoon olive oil
3	cloves garlic, minced
1/2	cup calamata olives, pitted and chopped
1	teaspoon fresh rosemary, chopped, or 1/2 teaspoon dried
1	teaspoon fresh thyme, or 1/2 teaspoon dried
1/3	cup white wine
1/2	cup grated Parmesan or feta cheese (optional)

Cook the penne according to package directions. Meanwhile, sauté the onion in olive oil until soft, about 5 minutes. Add the garlic, olives, rosemary, thyme, and wine and bring to a boil. Turn heat to low and simmer 3 to 4 minutes. Toss with pasta, and then with the cheese, if using.

Serves 4

Each serving provides:

494	Calories	83 g	Carbohydrate
14 g	Protein	527 mg	Sodium
11 g	Fat	8 mg	Cholesterol

Basil and Parmesan Ravioli

Preparation Time: 30 minutes

Does fresh ravioli made in 30 minutes seem impossible? Not anymore, when you consider the many places you can buy pre-made sheets of pasta or frozen wonton wrappers. As mentioned in the introduction to this chapter, many new upscale supermarkets and pasta shops make their own pasta and will sell you sheets of pasta at inexpensive prices. As a second choice, check for wonton wrappers in the freezer case. Homemade ravioli are always a wonderful first course or entree for a dinner party, and now they are quick to make.

1	pound fresh ravioli dough (see above) or 1 package frozen wonton wrappers
1	cup lowfat ricotta cheese
1	egg yolk, lightly beaten
1/2	cup Parmesan cheese, grated
2/3	cup fresh basil, chopped
2	tablespoons extra-virgin olive oil or a tomato, cream, or other sauce

Lay the dough or wonton wrappers out flat. In a bowl, mix the remaining ingredients, except the oil or sauce. Cut the dough into 3 × 5-inch pieces and place a tablespoon of the filling on one half (lengthwise). Fold over and seal using the tines of a fork and a little warm water spread along the edges with your finger. When finished, place the ravioli in gently boiling water (do not use rapidly boiling water since it may tear the ravioli apart) and cook for 3 to 4 minutes. Drain, drizzle with olive oil or sauce of your choice.

Makes 30 large ravioli

Each serving (5 ravioli) provides:

394	Calories	63 g	Carbohydrate
18 g	Protein	444 mg	Sodium
9 g	Fat	48 mg	Cholesterol

Ratatouille Pizza

PREPARATION TIME: 30 minutes

A quick pizza that will get your kids to love vegetables. Use a good-quality bread for best results—I prefer unbaked focaccia, available in many stores.

1	prepared focaccia bread or pizza crust
3	tablespoons olive oil
1	small onion, chopped
2	medium zucchinis, sliced
2	medium red peppers, seeded and sliced into thin strips
1	tablespoon dried basil
1	teaspoon dried oregano
1	teaspoon dried dill
3	cloves garlic, minced
	Parmesan cheese

Preheat oven to 400° or the temperature recommended for the packaged bread. Rub the bread with 1 tablespoon of the olive oil and set aside. Heat the remaining 2 tablespoons of olive oil in a skillet and add the onion, zucchini, and red pepper. Stir in the spices and sauté until soft, about 10 minutes. Add the garlic for the last half of cooking. Pour the vegetables over the bread and bake 10 to 15 minutes, or according to the package instructions. Sprinkle Parmesan on top for the last 4 to 5 minutes of cooking.

Serves 4

Each serving provides:

276	Calories	42 g	Carbohydrate
10 g	Protein	436 mg	Sodium
7 g	Fat	4 mg	Cholesterol

Penne with Peppers

PREPARATION TIME: 20 minutes

Colorful and full of flavor, this pasta goes especially well with a sweet salad.

1	red bell pepper, seeded and julienned
1	yellow bell pepper, seeded and julienned
1	green bell pepper, seeded and julienned
3	tablespoons olive oil
2	cloves garlic, minced
1	medium zucchini, sliced
2	teaspoons fresh thyme or 1 teaspoon dried
10	ounces penne or other hollow pasta
3/4	cup nonfat ricotta cheese
3/4	cup plain yogurt

Sauté peppers in the oil over low-medium heat for 2 to 3 minutes. Add garlic, zucchini, and thyme and sauté another 5 to 6 minutes. Cook the pasta according to package directions. Combine the cheese and yogurt in a blender and process until smooth. Stir the cheese into the pepper mixture and then toss with the pasta.

Serves 4

Each serving provides:

426	Calories	62 g	Carbohydrate
18 g	Protein	125 mg	Sodium
12 g	Fat	10 mg	Cholesterol

Bow-Tie Pasta with Mint

PREPARATION TIME: 20 minutes

Here's an easy dinner or first course that has a refreshingly simple taste. The heat comes from the abundance of garlic.

12	ounces farfalle (bow-tie) or other small pasta
1	tablespoon extra-virgin olive oil
2	shallots, minced
1	red or yellow bell pepper, chopped
2	cloves garlic, minced
2	zucchinis, sliced thin
1 1/2	tablespoons fresh mint, minced
1/3	cup fresh basil, chopped

Cook the pasta according to package directions and drain. Heat the oil and sauté the shallots and pepper until soft, about 6 minutes. Add the garlic and zucchini and heat until just warm. Remove from heat and stir in the mint and basil. Add mixture to pasta and toss.

Serves 4

Each serving provides:

350	Calories	65 g	Carbohydrate
11 g	Protein	8 mg	Sodium
5 g	Fat	0 mg	Cholesterol

Linguine with Lemon and Caramelized Fennel

PREPARATION TIME: 1 hour

The caramelized fennel is sweet and the lemon is sour, a good combination for an unusual pasta dish.

3	tablespoons extra-virgin olive oil
1	onion, halved and sliced thin
1	small fennel bulb, sliced thin
1	red pepper, cut into matchsticks
2	cloves garlic, minced or chopped
2	teaspoons lemon zest
1	tablespoon lemon juice
1	teaspoon jalapeño pepper, seeded and minced
1	pound linguine or other pasta

Heat 2 tablespoons of the oil in a saucepan and add the onion and fennel. Stir for 10 minutes over medium heat. Reduce heat and cook, stirring frequently, for 30 minutes. Add the red pepper and garlic and cook until onion and fennel are golden brown and caramelized, about 10 minutes more. Stir in the lemon zest and juice. Add hot pepper. Cook the pasta according to package directions, drain, and toss with the remaining tablespoon of olive oil and the onion mixture.

Serves 4 as a main course

Each serving provides:

571	Calories	98 g	Carbohydrate
16 g	Protein	26 mg	Sodium
12 g	Fat	0 mg	Cholesterol

Fettuccine with Garlic and Zucchini

PREPARATION TIME: 20 minutes

A quick, simple, and flavorful pasta with wonderful summer flavors. Serve with a green salad tossed with a vinaigrette.

2	medium zucchinis, julienned
2 1/2	tablespoons extra-virgin olive oil
4	cloves garlic, minced
1	pound fettuccine or other pasta
2	tablespoons fresh thyme or 1 tablespoon dried
	Parmesan cheese (optional)

Steam the zucchini until just tender. Heat the olive oil over low heat and add the garlic, cooking gently so it does not brown, about 10 minutes. Meanwhile, cook the pasta and drain. Toss with the other ingredients and top with Parmesan cheese, if desired.

Serves 4

Each serving provides:

533	Calories	92 g	Carbohydrate
16 g	Protein	6 mg	Sodium
11 g	Fat	0 mg	Cholesterol

Fettuccine with Peas and Peppers

PREPARATION TIME: 20 minutes

A rich pasta with plenty of color. You might consider a butter and oil mix for the sauté.

1	cup fresh peas or pea pods
4	tablespoons butter or vegetable oil
1/2	red bell pepper, seeded and julienned
4	mushrooms, sliced
12	ounces fettuccine
2	tablespoons half-and-half or cream
2	tablespoons fresh chives or scallions, minced
1/3	cup fresh Parmesan cheese, grated (optional)

Steam or microwave peas or pea pods until tender. Heat the butter or oil in a skillet and sauté pepper 2 to 3 minutes. Add the mushrooms and stir, heating for another 3 to 4 minutes until just cooked. Cook fettuccine according to package directions. Add the cream, chives, and Parmesan cheese, if using, to the fettuccine and mix well. Fold in the peas, peppers, and mushrooms.

Serves 4

Each serving provides:

492	Calories	75 g	Carbohydrate
14 g	Protein	130 mg	Sodium
15 g	Fat	36 mg	Cholesterol

Quick Lemon-Ricotta Ravioli

PREPARATION TIME: 30 minutes

I first made this pasta on a trip to the beach with friends. The beach house kitchen was tiny, but this dish was easy to make even in the cramped quarters, and it was a big hit.

1	pound fresh ravioli dough or 1 package frozen wonton wrappers (See Basil and Parmesan Ravioli, page 140, or introduction to this chapter, page 133, for fast dough or wonton wrappers.)
1 1/2	cups lowfat ricotta
2	egg yolks, lightly beaten
1	tablespoon lemon juice
	Zest from two lemons
2	tablespoons extra-virgin olive oil, or a tomato sauce
1	sprig fresh rosemary (optional)

Lay the dough or wonton wrappers out flat. In a bowl, mix the remaining ingredients, except the oil or sauce and rosemary. Cut the dough into 3 × 5-inch pieces and place a tablespoon of the filling on one half (lengthwise). Fold over and seal using the tines of a fork and a little warm water spread along the edges with your finger. When finished, place the ravioli in gently boiling water (do not use rapidly boiling water since it may tear the ravioli apart) and cook for 3 to 4 minutes. Warm the olive oil or sauce in a small skillet with the fresh rosemary, if using, for 5 minutes, stirring frequently. Remove the rosemary. Drain ravioli and drizzle the olive oil on top.

Makes 30 large ravioli

Each serving (5 ravioli) provides:

360	Calories	63 g	Carbohydrate
14 g	Protein	262 mg	Sodium
7 g	Fat	76 mg	Cholesterol

Peppers Stuffed with Pasta and Cheese

PREPARATION TIME: 20 minutes (plus 35 minutes baking time)

Orzo is superior to rice for stuffing since it maintains a little of its own flavor in process. All you need to serve with this is bread.

8   ounces orzo or other small pasta
6   large red or green sweet peppers
1/8   teaspoon salt
1/4   teaspoon pepper
1   tablespoon extra-virgin olive oil
1/2   cup calamata olives, pitted
1/4   cup parsley, chopped
2   teaspoons pine nuts
1/8   teaspoon Tabasco or other hot sauce
4   ounces goat cheese or cubed mozzarella

Preheat oven to 400°. Cook the pasta two-thirds of the time recommended on the package. Cut tops off the peppers and remove seeds and veins. Mix together the salt, pepper, and oil, then spread the mixture on the inside of the peppers. Chop the olives and mix with parsley and pine nuts. Drain the pasta and combine with olive mixture and hot sauce. Stir in cheese, then spoon the mix into the peppers. Place in an oiled or greased baking pan and cover with foil. Cook 10 minutes, remove foil, and cook another 25 minutes.

Serves 6

Each serving provides:

274	Calories	34 g	Carbohydrate
9 g	Protein	469 mg	Sodium
12 g	Fat	9 mg	Cholesterol

Mushroom–Ginger Pasta

PREPARATION TIME: 25 minutes

Ginger is good for you. It has been used for centuries in Asia and Africa for a variety of stomach ailments, and—guess what—Western science is beginning to agree that folk medicine works. I simply love the taste and smell of fresh ginger.

1	onion, cut in half and thinly sliced
1	tablespoon olive oil
1	pound mushrooms, sliced
$^1/_2$	cup dry white wine
1	cup nonfat sour cream
1	cup yogurt
2	teaspoons fresh ginger, grated
1	pound fettucine, cooked

Sauté the onion in oil for 3 minutes. Remove onions, then add mushrooms to the oil and sauté for another 4 to 5 minutes. Add the white wine, bring to a boil, then cook down to 3 to 4 tablespoons. Return onions to pan, then add sour cream, yogurt, and ginger and remove from heat. Mix well; toss with pasta.

Serves 4

Each serving provides:

603	Calories	108 g	Carbohydrate
25 g	Protein	86 mg	Sodium
7 g	Fat	4 mg	Cholesterol

Sicilian Pizza

PREPARATION TIME: 30 minutes

Some ready-to-bake pizza crusts and focaccia breads are very good and work well for pizza. You can also use a baguette— just slice it in half lengthwise and then into long pieces. Use a good bread and you'll love this pizza.

1	ready-to-bake pizza crust or focaccia bread
1/4	cup olive oil
1	pound eggplant, peeled and cut into small cubes
3	cloves garlic, minced
1/2	cup dry red wine
10	olives
1	teaspoon serrano or other hot pepper, seeded and minced
1/8	teaspoon salt
1/8	teaspoon pepper
1	tablespoon oregano
1	cup grated mozzarella cheese

Preheat oven to 450°. Rub the crust or bread with a little of the olive oil. Heat all but 2 to 3 tablespoons of the remaining olive oil and fry the eggplant and garlic over medium-low heat until the eggplant softens, about 8 minutes. Add the wine, olives, serrano, salt, and pepper and cook 3 to 4 minutes. Spread the filling over the bread and sprinkle with oregano and cheese. Drizzle the remaining olive oil on top. Bake about 15 minutes.

Serves 4

Each serving provides:

440	Calories	44 g	Carbohydrate
14 g	Protein	640 mg	Sodium
22 g	Fat	16 mg	Cholesterol

Roasted Tomato and Raw Vegetable Pasta

PREPARATION TIME: 20 minutes (plus 90 minutes
roasting time)

*If you are looking for an easy side dish, roasted tomatoes are
wonderful. Use the Roma tomatoes and figure they will lose
half their volume with slow roasting. This is a nice summer
combination of soft and crisp tastes.*

12	Roma tomatoes, halved
5	tablespoons extra-virgin olive oil
1/4	teaspoon dried rosemary
1/4	teaspoon dried thyme
1	pound fettuccine
2	cloves garlic, minced
2	tablespoons parsley, chopped
2	celery stalks, chopped
1	bell pepper, preferably yellow, sliced
1/2	teaspoon jalapeño or other hot pepper, seeded and minced
1/2	cup Parmesan cheese, grated (optional)

Preheat oven to 300°. Rub the tomatoes with 1 tablespoon of the olive oil, sprinkle the herbs over them, then place face down on a baking sheet. Bake for 1 hour, push them around with a wooden spoon to prevent sticking, and continue to cook for another 90 minutes. Cook the pasta according to package directions, drain. Combine the remaining 4 tablespoons of olive oil with the rest of the ingredients in a bowl, add the pasta and tomatoes, and toss.

Serves 4 to 6

Each serving provides:

433	Calories	68 g	Carbohydrate
12 g	Protein	26 mg	Sodium
13 g	Fat	0 mg	Cholesterol

Spaghetti with Hot Pepper Sauce

PREPARATION TIME: 25 minutes

Turning oil into pepper oil is simple with a jalapeño. If you happen to have hot pepper oil on hand, just use that and forget making your own.

12	ounces spaghetti
7	mushrooms, sliced
1/2	sweet red pepper, seeded and julienned
5	tablespoons extra-virgin olive oil
4	cloves garlic, minced
1	jalapeño, seeded and sliced
2	tablespoons fresh parsley, chopped

Cook the spaghetti according to package directions. Meanwhile, sauté the mushroom and sweet pepper in 1 tablespoon of the oil until soft, about 8 minutes. In a separate saucepan, heat the remaining 4 tablespoons oil with the garlic and hot pepper and cook on medium-low heat for about 8 minutes. Discard the hot pepper, then mix the oil with the mushrooms and sweet peppers. Add this mixture to the pasta and toss with parsley.

Serves 4

Each serving provides:

474	Calories	72 g	Carbohydrate
13 g	Protein	6 mg	Sodium
15 g	Fat	0 mg	Cholesterol

Penne with Broccoli

PREPARATION TIME: 20 minutes

Make sure you don't overcook the broccoli for this dish—you want it to have some crunch. If you like, sauté a little red pepper and toss it with the pasta as well.

12	ounces penne or macaroni
1	small onion, cut in half and thinly sliced
3	cloves garlic, minced
2	tablespoons extra-virgin olive oil
1/4	cup pine nuts
1	pound broccoli, chopped
1/8	teaspoon salt
1/4	teaspoon pepper
	Parmesan cheese (optional)

Cook the pasta according to package directions. Sauté the onion and garlic in oil over medium-low heat for 6 to 7 minutes. Add the pine nuts. Steam the broccoli until crisp-tender. Toss all with the pasta except cheese. Serve the Parmesan cheese on the side.

Serves 4

~~~~~~~~~~~~~~~~

Each serving provides:

482	Calories	76 g	Carbohydrate
17 g	Protein	91 mg	Sodium
14 g	Fat	0 mg	Cholesterol

Asparagus and Leek Pasta

Preparation Time: 20 minutes

This is especially great when the vegetables are grilled, but it is good even if you cook or steam the vegetables. With bread it makes a complete dinner.

2	leeks, white and light green parts, cleaned and sliced not quite all the way through lengthwise
1	pound asparagus, trimmed
1	tablespoon extra-virgin olive oil
1	pound penne or other pasta
1/4	teaspoon salt
1/4	teaspoon pepper
1 1/2	tablespoons parsley, minced
	Parmesan cheese (optional)

Coat the leeks and asparagus with the oil and place over an indoor or outdoor grill over medium-high heat. Cook until wilted and slightly browned. Let vegetables cool, then mince the leeks. (As an alternative, slice the leeks and cook in 2 tablespoons of oil in a skillet for about 10 minutes. Steam or microwave the asparagus). Cook the pasta according to package directions and drain. Cut the cooked asparagus into 2-inch pieces. Toss the pasta with all of the ingredients and serve. Sprinkle with cheese, if desired.

Serves 4

Each serving provides:

477	Calories	91 g	Carbohydrate
16 g	Protein	155 mg	Sodium
6 g	Fat	0 mg	Cholesterol

Ziti with Herbs

PREPARATION TIME: 15 minutes

I learned my lesson about hot peppers several years ago. Thinking I had rinsed my hands well enough, I went on about my cooking and happened to rub the corner of my eye a few minutes later. After 15 minutes of dousing my eye with cold water I began to recover. Use gloves with these peppers—they are among the hottest!

1	pound ziti, macaroni, or other pasta
2	Scotch bonnet or other hot pepper, whole (see Pepper Chart, page 8)
1/4	cup extra-virgin olive oil
1/4	cup fresh parsley, chopped
1/4	cup fresh basil, chopped or torn into pieces
3	tablespoons fresh thyme and/or rosemary or 1 1/2 teaspoons dried
	Parmesan cheese (optional)

Bring water to boil and add the pasta and the whole peppers. Gently heat the olive oil. When the pasta is just about done, stir the herbs into the olive oil. Drain pasta and discard the peppers. (Caution: If peppers happen to split during cooking, make sure the extremely hot seeds are not in the pasta.) Toss the herbs and oil with the pasta. Top with grated Parmesan cheese if desired.

Serves 4

Each serving provides:

576	Calories	92 g	Carbohydrate
16 g	Protein	8 mg	Sodium
16 g	Fat	0 mg	Cholesterol

Spaghetti Verdura

PREPARATION TIME: 20 minutes

This mix uses mustard to give the sauce a dressing effect. The shallots give it a rich flavor.

3	shallots, minced
1	clove garlic, minced
3	tablespoons extra-virgin olive oil
2	tablespoons Dijon mustard
2	zucchinis, cut in half lengthwise, then sliced
$1/2$	pound asparagus, cut into 1-inch pieces
1	pound spaghetti, cooked
2	tablespoons scallions or chives, chopped
$1/8$	teaspoon pepper

Sauté the shallots and garlic in 1 tablespoon of the oil until soft, about 5 minutes. Add remaining 2 tablespoons oil and mustard and mix well. Steam or microwave the zucchini and asparagus until crisp-tender. Toss the cooked pasta with the dressing to coat, then add vegetables and scallions and toss again. Season with pepper.

Serves 4

Each serving provides:

348	Calories	51 g	Carbohydrate
10 g	Protein	209 mg	Sodium
12 g	Fat	0 mg	Cholesterol

Spicy Gemelli with Radicchio, Olives, and Tomato

PREPARATION TIME: 25 minutes

Gemelli is a short, round pasta that works well with this dish, but you can use whatever you have on hand. If you don't have the hot pepper oil, you can substitute extra-virgin olive oil.

1	pound gemelli or other pasta
1	tablespoon extra-virgin olive oil
1	tablespoon hot pepper oil or extra-virgin olive oil
3	cups small to medium size tomatoes, halved and sliced thin
1	clove garlic, minced
1	small head radicchio, trimmed and shredded
2	tablespoons parsley, chopped
2	tablespoons calamata olives, chopped
1/8	teaspoon pepper

Cook the pasta according to package directions and reserve 1/4 cup of the cooking water. Heat the oils in a skillet and add the tomatoes and garlic. Heat through, about 4 minutes, then add the radicchio and water used to cook the pasta. Heat until radicchio is wilted, about 2 minutes, then toss with the pasta, parsley, olives, and pepper.

Serves 4

Each serving provides:

556	Calories	97 g	Carbohydrate
17 g	Protein	213 mg	Sodium
12 g	Fat	0 mg	Cholesterol

Penne with Walnuts and Basil

PREPARATION TIME: 30 minutes

This dish is a little higher in fat but has a rich taste with just a little bit of spice.

1/4 cup walnuts
1 tablespoon vegetable oil
1 clove garlic, minced
1/2 teaspoon hot pepper, minced
(see Pepper Chart, page 8)
1 1/4 tablespoons flour
3/4 cup half-and-half or cream
1/4 cup dry sherry
1/8 teaspoon salt
12 ounces penne or other small pasta
1/3 cup fresh basil, chopped, or 1 1/2 tablespoons dried
1/3 cup Parmesan cheese, grated
Ground pepper (optional)

Place the walnuts in a dry skillet over medium heat and toast for 3 to 5 minutes, or until they begin to release their fragrance. Remove from skillet and set aside. Heat the oil in the skillet and sauté the garlic and pepper for 2 minutes over medium heat, then add the flour and stir over medium-high heat until combined. Add the half-and-half, sherry, and salt, and cook until the sauce has thickened, about 10 to 15 minutes. Cook the pasta according to package directions and drain. Remove the sauce from the heat and stir in the basil and Parmesan. Top with pepper if desired.

Serves 4

Each serving provides:

492	Calories	66 g	Carbohydrate
16 g	Protein	246 mg	Sodium
16 g	Fat	30 mg	Cholesterol

Fresh Tomato Fettuccine

PREPARATION TIME: 20 minutes

This pasta dish is a perfect way to add a spicy touch to fresh summer tomatoes. For peeling and seeding the tomatoes, see Introduction, page 4.

1	pound fettuccine, cooked
6	ripe tomatoes, peeled, seeded, and chopped
1	cup fresh basil leaves, chopped
1/2	cup fresh parsley, chopped
2	tablespoons extra-virgin olive oil
5	cloves garlic, minced
1	tablespoon jalapeño or serrano, seeded and minced

Cook the fettuccine according to package directions. Meanwhile, combine the tomatoes, basil, and parsley in a bowl. Heat the oil over medium-low heat and add the garlic. Sauté until just soft, 3 to 4 minutes, then add pepper and sauté another minute. Add to the tomato mixture, then toss all with the pasta.

Serves 4

Each serving provides:

553	Calories	100 g	Carbohydrate
17 g	Protein	32 mg	Sodium
10 g	Fat	0 mg	Cholesterol

Asian "Pesto" Pasta

PREPARATION TIME: 20 minutes

This flavorful sauce brings the ginger and soy flavors to a traditional Italian pesto sauce.

20   basil leaves
1 1/2 cups fresh cilantro leaves, chopped
2   tablespoons fresh ginger, grated
2   teaspoons tamari or soy sauce
1   tablespoon white wine vinegar
1   teaspoon hot pepper, seeded and minced (see Pepper Chart, page 8)
2   cloves garlic, minced
1/4   cup peanut oil
1/4   cup unsalted peanuts (optional)
1   pound linguine or other pasta, cooked

Combine all ingredients except pasta in blender or food processor and puree. Toss with the pasta.

Serves 4

Each serving provides:

576	Calories	92 g	Carbohydrate
16 g	Protein	188 mg	Sodium
16 g	Fat	0 mg	Cholesterol

Sweet Pepper Cannelloni

PREPARATION TIME: 30 minutes (plus 20 minutes baking time)

This is great with fresh pasta but it works just fine with dried pasta, too.

1/2	pound ricotta cheese
4	ounces mozzarella cheese, shredded
3/4	cup chopped roasted red pepper, jarred okay
1	egg, lightly beaten
3	tablespoons parsley, chopped
1/4	teaspoon salt or to taste
1/4	teaspoon pepper or to taste
1/4	cup grated Parmesan cheese
1/2	pound cannelloni or manicotti (or use fresh pasta sheets—see introduction to this chapter, page 133—and lay flat, fill, then cut and roll)
1 1/2	cups Very Fast Tomato Sauce (page 25) or tomato sauce of your choice

Preheat oven to 375°. Bring a large pot of water to a boil.
Combine the ricotta, mozzarella, pepper, egg, parsley, salt,
pepper, and half of the Parmesan cheese and set aside.
Cook the pasta according to package instructions but un-
dercook slightly. Place cooked pasta in cold water to stop
cooking, then fill each piece with cheese mixture. Spread
a little of the tomato sauce on the bottom of a lightly oiled
baking dish. Place the filled pasta inside, then pour the rest
of the tomato sauce on top and sprinkle the remaining
Parmesan. Bake about 20 minutes.

Serves 6

Each serving provides:

321	Calories	40 g	Carbohydrate
17 g	Protein	684 mg	Sodium
10 g	Fat	55 mg	Cholesterol

Hazelnut, Mascarpone, and Gorgonzola Ravioli

PREPARATION TIME: 30 minutes

I made this ravioli for a dinner party; however, once I tasted the filling there were fewer ravioli available. This is not a lowfat ravioli, but it is so wonderful I just couldn't help but include it. Olive oil, or a spicy or regular tomato sauce, may be used on this.

1/4	cup hazelnuts, minced
6	ounces Gorgonzola cheese, in pieces
3/4	cup mascarpone cheese
1	pound fresh ravioli dough or 1 package frozen wonton wrappers (See Basil and Parmesan Ravioli, page 140 or introduction to this chapter, page 133, for fast dough or wonton wrappers.)
2	tablespoons extra-virgin olive oil or sauce of your choice

Place the hazelnuts in a dry skillet over medium heat and toast for 3 to 4 minutes, stirring constantly. Remove from heat and combine well with cheeses.

Lay the dough or wonton wrappers out flat. Cut the dough into 3 × 5-inch pieces and place a tablespoon of the filling on one half (lengthwise). Fold over and seal using the tines of a fork and a little warm water spread along the edges with your finger. When finished, place the ravioli in gently boiling water (do not use rapidly boiling water since it may tear the ravioli apart) and cook for 3 to 4 minutes. Drain, drizzle olive oil on top.

Makes 30 large ravioli

Each serving (5 ravioli) provides:

505	Calories	62 g	Carbohydrate
17 g	Protein	533 mg	Sodium
22 g	Fat	63 mg	Cholesterol

6

Main
Dishes

For many people, the idea of vegetarian main dishes conjures up what they're missing instead of what they have. I suppose that's to be expected when the term "meatless" is used. Yet we don't think of ourselves as missing something when we order Bok Choy with Black Mushrooms, Fettuccine Alfredo, or even Macaroni and Cheese in a restaurant. Why then, when cooking at home, do we think that eating vegetarian means "missing" something?

As promised in the introduction to this book, there is no tofu in these entrees. Personally, I think tofu has gotten a bad rap—it is a high protein food which absorbs the flavors around it very well. But the resistance is out there, so for those who are not vegetarian, but want to eat less meat, here you will find comforting signposts of old familiar ingredients as you travel along this new path to healthful eating. These dishes, I believe, will serve you well.

Vegetable Stir-Fry with Ginger Sauce

PREPARATION TIME: 25 minutes

The flavor of this sweet sauce is delightful over vegetables and rice. It seems like it should take longer to make for as good as it tastes. I've listed my favorite mix of vegetables, but substitute with what's in season and what you have on hand: carrots, broccoli, etc.

6	tablespoons rice vinegar
5	tablespoons sugar
3/4	cup plus $1^1/2$ tablespoons water
1	tablespoon cornstarch
2	tablespoons tamari or soy sauce
1	tablespoon fresh ginger, grated
2	tablespoons vegetable oil
1	red pepper, seeded and julienned
1	onion, cut in half and thinly sliced
2	cloves garlic, minced
8	mushrooms, sliced
2	zucchinis, sliced
5	cups cooked rice

Bring the vinegar, sugar, and the 3/4 cup of water to a boil. Reduce heat and simmer 5 minutes. Mix the cornstarch with the $1^1/2$ tablespoons of water, then stir it into the sauce. Add tamari or soy sauce and cook until thickened, about 5 minutes. Remove from heat and stir in the ginger.

In a skillet, heat the oil over medium-high heat and stir-fry the vegetables until crisp-tender. Cook the pepper and the onion for 2 minutes, then add the garlic, mushrooms, and zucchini for 4 to 5 minutes. Spread the vegetables over the rice. Top with the sauce.

Serves 4

Each serving provides:

504	Calories	98 g	Carbohydrate
10 g	Protein	516 mg	Sodium
8 g	Fat	0 mg	Cholesterol

Chile Pepper and Sour Cream Quesadillas

PREPARATION TIME: 20 minutes

Quick and easy to make, these quesadillas use ingredients we usually have on hand. A nice lunch.

1	tablespoon vegetable oil
1	to 2 jalapeños, seeded and minced
1	bell pepper, red or green, seeded and cut into strips
1/2	small onion, thinly sliced
4	flour tortillas
1	cup lowfat Monterey Jack or Cheddar cheese, shredded
1	cup nonfat sour cream

Heat the oil in a skillet and add the peppers and onion. Cook over medium heat until softened, about 8 minutes. Place one tortilla in a dry skillet or on a griddle over medium heat.

Spread one fourth of the cheese along one side, then top with one fourth of the pepper-onion mixture. Fold over with a spatula, cook 30 seconds, turn and cook a few seconds more. Remove and repeat with other three tortillas. Serve with sour cream.

Makes 4 quesadillas

Each serving provides:

367	Calories	42 g	Carbohydrate
19 g	Protein	322 mg	Sodium
13 g	Fat	20 mg	Cholesterol

Sweet & Sour & Spicy

PREPARATION TIME: 20 minutes

Without the jalapeño this dish is pretty close to a sweet & sour stir-fry. The hot pepper gives it a spicy boost. Serve over rice.

$1/4$ cup catsup
$1/8$ cup soy sauce
$1/3$ cup cider vinegar
$1/3$ cup brown sugar
$1/2$ cup water
2   tablespoons cornstarch dissolved in 2 tablespoons of water
2   tablespoons vegetable oil
1   small onion, cut in half and thinly sliced
2   cloves garlic, minced
1   jalapeño or serrano, seeded and finely chopped
1   red bell pepper, seeded and julienned
1   green bell pepper, seeded and julienned
1   small zucchini, diced
3   mushrooms, sliced

Mix the first 6 ingredients together in a small saucepan to make the sweet & sour sauce warm. In a skillet, heat the vegetable oil and sauté onion for 3 to 4 minutes, then add garlic and peppers and stir-fry another 3 to 4 minutes. Add zucchini and mushrooms and stir-fry until mushrooms begin to color. Add the sauce and stir another minute. Remove from heat and serve.

Serves 4

Each serving provides:

208	Calories	36 g	Carbohydrate
2 g	Protein	705 mg	Sodium
7 g	Fat	0 mg	Cholesterol

Vegetarian Burritos

PREPARATION TIME: 30 minutes

We enjoy a variety of vegetarian burritos since tortillas lend themselves to many creations. This one is a favorite—you won't miss the meat.

1	onion, finely chopped
1	red or green bell pepper, seeded and finely chopped
1	jalapeño, seeded and finely chopped
1	tablespoon vegetable oil
1	teaspoon ground cumin
2	cloves garlic, minced
1	cup black beans, canned okay (see Introduction, page 3)
1	small zucchini, diced
6	to 8 flour tortillas
	Cheddar or Monterey Jack cheese (optional)
	Shredded iceberg lettuce
	Salsa
	Sour cream (optional)

Sauté the onion and peppers in oil until soft, about 7 minutes. Add the cumin, garlic, black beans, and zucchini and sauté for about 6 minutes more, until the zucchini is cooked but still crisp. Heat the tortillas in a dry skillet until just warm, or place in a microwave, cover loosely with a paper towel, and heat for 40 seconds. Place filling in each tortilla, top with sprinkled cheese, if using, and place under the broiler until the cheese melts. Sprinkle with shredded lettuce and serve with salsa and sour cream if desired.

Serves 4

Each serving provides:

415	Calories	63 g	Carbohydrate
14 g	Protein	252 mg	Sodium
11 g	Fat	0 mg	Cholesterol

Three-Pepper Chili

PREPARATION TIME: 20 minutes (plus 25 minutes cooking time)

A nice, warming mixture of beans and peppers, this is a spicy chili you'll want to serve with cornbread on the side.

1	tablespoon olive oil
1	cup red bell pepper, seeded and chopped
1/2	cup Anaheim or other mild pepper, seeded and chopped
2	tablespoons jalapeño, seeded and minced
1/2	cup onion, chopped
3	cloves garlic
1	tablespoon ground cumin
1	tablespoon chili powder
2	teaspoons paprika
1/2	cup pineapple juice
1	28-ounce can Italian-style plum tomatoes with juice, chopped
1	15-ounce can red kidney beans, rinsed and drained
1	15-ounce can white kidney beans (cannellini beans), rinsed and drained
1	15-ounce can black beans, rinsed and drained

Heat the olive oil and sauté the peppers, onion, and garlic over low heat until soft, about 8 minutes. Stir in the spices, then add the remaining ingredients and bring to a boil. Simmer 25 minutes, adding water if needed.

Serves 6

Each serving provides:

241	Calories	43 g	Carbohydrate
12 g	Protein	735 mg	Sodium
4 g	Fat	0 mg	Cholesterol

Spicy Shish Kabobs

PREPARATION TIME: 30 minutes

Why should shish kabobs be limited to the carnivores? Shiitake mushrooms, if available, are meatier than other mushrooms and hold up to barbecuing a little better.

2	tablespoons olive oil
1/2	onion, finely chopped
1/2	sweet pepper, seeded and finely chopped
1	stalk celery, finely chopped
2	cloves garlic, minced
1/4	teaspoon paprika
1/2	teaspoon ground coriander
1/8	teaspoon cayenne pepper
1/8	teaspoon chili powder
1/2	teaspoon dried basil
1	teaspoon fresh thyme or 1/2 teaspoon dried
1/8	teaspoon pepper
1/2	cup vegetable broth or water
1/2	cup tomato sauce
1/8	teaspoon Tabasco or other hot sauce
3	zucchinis, cut into 1/2-inch slices
1	pound cherry tomatoes
8	to 10 mushrooms (shiitake, cremini, or button)
4	sweet peppers, seeded and cut into squares

Heat the oil in a skillet, then add onion, chopped pepper, celery, and garlic. Add the seasonings and mix well. Sauté over medium-low heat, stirring occasionally, until onion and peppers are soft, about 8 minutes. Add broth or water, tomato sauce, and Tabasco, increase to a boil, then simmer uncovered until sauce thickens, about 15 minutes. Preheat a charcoal fire or broiler and thread the vegetables onto a skewer. Brush them with the sauce so that all sides are well coated. If broiling, place in a dish and broil for about 5 minutes, turning frequently. If grilling, place over medium-hot coals and grill about 5 minutes on each side.

Serves 4

Each serving provides:

154	Calories	21 g	Carbohydrate
4 g	Protein	217 mg	Sodium
8 g	Fat	0 mg	Cholesterol

Mushroom and Cilantro Tostadas

PREPARATION TIME: 30 minutes

Tostadas are frequently my answer to a quick dinner. I like the crunch of the tortilla with a variety of toppings.

1/4	cup vegetable oil
6	corn tortillas
1/4	cup onion, finely diced
2	tablespoons jalapeño, seeded and finely diced
1/4	cup red or green pepper, seeded and finely diced
2	cloves garlic, minced
1	pound mushrooms (cremini or button), sliced
3	tablespoons cilantro, finely chopped
	Salsa
	Sour cream (optional)

In a skillet, heat the vegetable oil until hot, then add tortillas one at a time. Fry the tortillas, turning once, until crisp, about a minute on each side. Drain on paper towel and set aside. Rinse the skillet of all but 3 tablespoons of oil, and sauté the onion and peppers until just soft, about 5 minutes. Add the garlic and sauté another minute. Add mushrooms and cilantro and cook until mushrooms have softened, about 7 minutes. Scoop the mushroom mixture onto the tortilla and serve with salsa and sour cream, if desired, on top.

Makes 6 tostadas

Each tostada provides:

186	Calories	22 g	Carbohydrate
4 g	Protein	219 mg	Sodium
10 g	Fat	0 mg	Cholesterol

Caramelized Shallot, Mushroom, and Fennel Quesadillas

PREPARATION TIME: 40 minutes

These make a nice meal by themselves, and have a wonderfully rich taste. Serve with rice (these are good with either tamarind rice or fruit rice) or a salad.

1	tablespoon butter
1 1/2	tablespoons olive oil
1/2	pound mushrooms, washed and thickly sliced
8	shallots, peeled and sliced
1	jalapeño pepper, seeded and chopped
1	fennel bulb, thinly sliced
1	teaspoon sugar
1/2	cup white wine
	Chopped parsley (optional)
4	flour tortillas
	Monterey Jack or Cheddar cheese (optional)

In a small skillet, heat half of the butter and oil and add the mushrooms. Stir to coat, then cover and cook over medium heat for 25 minutes. Meanwhile, heat the remaining butter and oil in another small skillet and cook the shallots, pepper, and fennel, stirring often, for 15 minutes over medium heat. Add the sugar and cook another 8 minutes. Add the wine, bring to a boil, and cook until the liquid has evaporated and the vegetables are soft. Remove from heat and stir in the mushrooms and parsley, if using. Spread one fourth of the filling down one side of a tortilla, place in a large skillet or griddle, and heat. After 30 seconds, sprinkle cheese on top, if using, and fold over and continue to warm for another 30 seconds. Repeat for the other three tortillas.

Serves 4

Each serving provides:

343	Calories	46 g	Carbohydrate
9 g	Protein	129 mg	Sodium
13 g	Fat	8 mg	Cholesterol

Mexican Stuffed Peppers

PREPARATION TIME: 35 minutes (plus 30 minutes baking time)

Stuffed, sweet peppers with a spicy filling make a great dinner.
Try a salad with a cilantro-infused vinaigrette on the side.

1	onion, chopped
1	jalapeño, seeded and minced
1	tablespoon vegetable or olive oil
2	cloves garlic, minced
1	tablespoon good-quality chili powder
$^1/_2$	teaspoon cumin
$1^1/_4$	cups rice
1	15-ounce can tomatoes, with juice
2	cups vegetable broth or water
4	red or green bell peppers, cored and seeded
	Parmesan or Cheddar cheese (optional)

Preheat oven to 350°. Sauté the onion and jalapeño in oil until
soft, then add garlic, chili powder, and cumin. Stir in rice and
cook, stirring, until golden, 4 to 5 minutes. Add the tomatoes
and broth or water, bring to a boil, then cover and reduce heat.
Simmer 25 minutes.

Meanwhile, blanch the peppers in boiling water for 5 minutes and drain. Place peppers in a baking dish. Spoon rice mixture into peppers. Place the baking dish into another pan with $1/2$ inch of water, cover lightly with foil, and bake 30 minutes. If desired, grate Parmesan or Cheddar cheese on top and cook uncovered for an additional 5 minutes or until lightly browned.

Serves 4

Each serving provides:

324	Calories	64 g	Carbohydrate
7 g	Protein	210 mg	Sodium
5 g	Fat	0 mg	Cholesterol

Fiery Zucchini Casserole

PREPARATION TIME: 25 minutes

This quick casserole is strictly a stovetop dish, and it is a complete meal. To cool it off, cut down on the red pepper flakes.

1	onion, chopped
2	tablespoons vegetable or olive oil
4	zucchinis, thinly sliced
1	clove garlic, minced
2	medium tomatoes, peeled, with juice, or 1 (14-ounce) can with juice
1/2	teaspoon red pepper flakes
1/8	teaspoon ground cayenne
1 1/2	cups cooked rice

Sauté the onion in oil until soft, about 5 minutes. Add zucchini and sauté another 3 to 4 minutes. Add remaining ingredients, cover, and simmer about 15 minutes.

Serves 4

Each serving provides:

220	Calories	34 g	Carbohydrate
5 g	Protein	10 mg	Sodium
8 g	Fat	0 mg	Cholesterol

Vegetable-Pepper Casserole

PREPARATION TIME: 15 minutes (plus 25 minutes baking time)

This is a quick casserole supper with a warm mix of vegetables and spices.

1	onion, chopped
1	serrano, seeded and minced
2	cloves garlic, minced
1	tablespoon olive oil
2 1/2	cups cooked rice
2	zucchinis, shredded
2	tomatoes, peeled and chopped
1/4	cup Parmesan cheese, freshly grated
2	tablespoons vegetable broth or water
2	teaspoons fresh oregano or 1 teaspoon dried

Preheat oven to 350°. Sauté the onion, pepper, and garlic in the oil over low heat until soft, then combine with remaining ingredients in a baking dish and bake for 25 minutes.

Serves 4

Each serving provides:

274	Calories	48 g	Carbohydrate
8 g	Protein	104 mg	Sodium
6 g	Fat	4 mg	Cholesterol

Black Bean One-Skillet Casserole

PREPARATION TIME: 35 minutes

The black beans really aren't the star here—the spices and serrano are. And since this is not "pan-intensive," clean-up is a snap.

1	tablespoon olive oil
1	onion, chopped
1	large carrot, finely chopped
1	serrano, seeded and minced
3	cloves garlic, minced
2	cups black beans (see Introduction, page 3)
1/4	cup vegetable broth or water
2	tablespoons ground coriander
1/2	teaspoon dried marjoram
1/2	cup Cheddar cheese, grated

Preheat oven to 350°. Heat oil and sauté the onion, carrots, pepper, and garlic for 4 to 5 minutes. Add remaining ingredients except the cheese, and sauté for another 1 to 2 minutes. Bake 10 minutes, then cover with cheese, and bake another 5 to 10 minutes.

Serves 4

Each serving provides:

240	Calories	31 g	Carbohydrate
12 g	Protein	561 mg	Sodium
9 g	Fat	14 mg	Cholesterol

Mex-Italian Frittata

PREPARATION TIME: 35 minutes (includes making the sauce)

This zucchini frittata, a la Italy, is covered with a green sauce common in Mexican foods. In fact, you can use any extra sauce for enchiladas the next night.

4   medium zucchinis, cubed
2   tablespoons olive oil
1   teaspoon jalapeño, seeded and minced
6   large eggs
1/4 cup Monterey Jack cheese
     Mexican Green Sauce (page 26)

Sauté the zucchini in 1 tablespoon of the olive oil for about 10 minutes, add the pepper to the skillet, sauté for a minute or two longer, then remove from heat.

Beat the eggs and mix with the cheese. Add zucchini mixture to the eggs and stir. Heat the second tablespoon of olive oil in the pan over medium heat and pour the egg mixture in. Reduce heat to low and cook slowly until almost set in the middle. Remove and turn (or place under a broiler to finish cooking the other side). Pour Green Sauce over the frittata and serve.

Serves 4

Each serving not including Green Sauce provides:

218	Calories	5 g	Carbohydrate
13 g	Protein	136 mg	Sodium
17 g	Fat	326 mg	Cholesterol

Colorful Couscous Casserole

PREPARATION TIME: 20 minutes (plus 25 minutes baking time)

As pretty on the plate as it is delightful on the palate, this dish has a nice, spicy bite. You can serve a little Harissa (page 18) on the side if you wish.

1	tablespoon vegetable oil
1/2	onion, chopped
1/2	bell pepper, seeded and chopped
2	tablespoons jalapeño or serrano pepper, seeded and minced
1 1/2	cups water
1	cup couscous, uncooked
2	cups black beans, drained (see Introduction, page 3)
1/4	cup sliced water chestnuts
1	cup lowfat ricotta cheese
2	tablespoons rice vinegar
2	teaspoons peanut oil
1/4	teaspoon cayenne pepper

Preheat oven to 350°. Heat oil in a skillet and sauté the onion and peppers until soft, about 5 minutes. Heat water to a boil, remove from heat, and stir in the couscous. Cover and let stand until couscous is tender and water absorbed, about 5 minutes. Stir in black beans, onion, peppers, and water chestnuts. In a separate bowl, combine remaining ingredients then stir into the couscous mixture. Lightly coat a baking dish with oil or butter, spoon in the mixture, and bake, uncovered, for 25 minutes.

Serves 4

Each serving provides:

439	Calories	63 g	Carbohydrate
21 g	Protein	547 mg	Sodium
12 g	Fat	19 mg	Cholesterol

Andrew's Mushroom Ta-Rito

PREPARATION TIME: 20 minutes

My teenager Andrew is a big fan of these. I don't know if this qualifies as a taco or a burrito, so I just call it a ta-rito. Serve with rice or beans or both.

3	tablespoons vegetable oil
1	onion, chopped
2	cloves garlic, minced
1	pound mushrooms, thinly sliced
2	jalapeños, seeded and minced
1	14-ounce can tomatoes, drained and chopped, or 3/4 pound fresh
2	tablespoons fresh cilantro, chopped
1/4	pound Monterey Jack or Cheddar cheese, grated
6	flour tortillas
	Fresh salsa (optional)

Heat oil in a skillet and add onion and garlic. Sauté for 2 to 3 minutes, then add the mushrooms and peppers. Sauté another 3 to 4 minutes, add tomatoes, and sauté 10 minutes. Remove from heat and stir in the cilantro and cheese. Heat the tortillas in a dry skillet or microwave, then spoon in the filling, fold over, and top with salsa.

Makes 6 ta-ritos

Each ta-rito serving provides:

326	Calories	40 g	Carbohydrate
10 g	Protein	107 mg	Sodium
14 g	Fat	5 mg	Cholesterol

Hot & Spicy Fried Rice

PREPARATION TIME: 25 minutes

This quick rice dish goes well with a variety of foods, or is a complete and colorful dinner on its own.

4	cups cooked rice, cold
3	tablespoons peanut or corn oil
1	onion, diced
1	carrot, diced
1 1/2	small red bell peppers, seeded and diced
1/4	teaspoon dried red pepper flakes
3	scallions, thinly sliced

Separate the chilled rice with a fork. Heat a skillet or wok over medium-high heat until hot, add the oil and swirl to coat the pan. Add the onion and toss until hot, about 2 minutes. Reduce heat to medium, add the carrot and pepper, and toss for another 2 to 3 minutes. Stir in the rice and red pepper flakes. Remove from heat and stir in the scallions.

Serves 4

~~~~~~~~~~

Each serving provides:

388	Calories	65 g	Carbohydrate
7 g	Protein	12 mg	Sodium
11 g	Fat	0 mg	Cholesterol

Ginger, Daikon, and Sweet Pepper Tostadas

PREPARATION TIME: 40 minutes

This East-West blend of flavors is appropriately topped with an herb known as cilantro in the West and Chinese parsley in the East. I suggest you serve with a staple in both areas: rice.

1	tablespoon vegetable oil
1/2	teaspoon *each* ground cumin, coriander, chile pepper, and dried sage
1	sweet red or yellow pepper, sliced
1	jalapeño pepper, seeded and chopped
2	tablespoons fresh ginger, grated
4	corn tortillas
1 1/2	cups bok choy, finely chopped
3/4	cup diced daikon, or radish
1/2	cup minced pineapple
	Monterey Jack or Cheddar cheese (optional)
1/2	cup cilantro, chopped

Warm the oil in a skillet and stir in the spices. Add the peppers and ginger and cook until just slightly softened, about 5 minutes. Remove and set aside. Add more oil, if needed, to the pan to just cover the bottom and raise heat to medium-high. Fry 1 tortilla for a minute, then turn and cook for another 30 seconds or until crisp. Dry the tortilla with paper towels. Repeat with remaining tortillas. Cover each tortilla with a layer of bok choy and daikon. Add the pepper mixture and then the pineapple, topping with cheese, if desired, and cilantro.

Serves 4

Each serving provides:

557	Calories	118 g	Carbohydrate
16 g	Protein	551 mg	Sodium
7 g	Fat	0 mg	Cholesterol

Mexican "Quiche"

PREPARATION TIME: 20 minutes (plus 25 minutes baking time)

Perfect with a salad, or try it with Quick Mexican Vegetables (page 103).

4	corn tortillas
	Vegetable oil
3	tablespoons flour
$1/2$	teaspoon good-quality chili powder
$1/8$	teaspoon salt
1	medium tomato, chopped
2	tablespoons jalapeño, seeded and minced
4	to 5 green onions, sliced
$1/3$	cup salsa
3	eggs, beaten
$1/2$	cup milk
$1/2$	cup Monterey Jack or Cheddar cheese, grated

Preheat oven to 350°. Warm the tortillas in a dry skillet until soft, then coat an 11- × 8- × 2-inch baking dish with the oil and arrange the tortillas to cover. In a bowl, combine the flour, chili powder, and salt. Sprinkle the tortillas with a little of the flour mixture. Top with the tomato, pepper, and onion. Sprinkle again with the flour mixture. Spoon salsa over the top. Combine the eggs and milk well and pour over the vegetables. Bake, uncovered, about 20 to 25 minutes or until a toothpick inserted comes out clean. Top with cheese and bake until cheese melts.

Serves 4

Each serving provides:

239	Calories	25 g	Carbohydrate
12 g	Protein	386 mg	Sodium
10 g	Fat	175 mg	Cholesterol

Curried Vegetables

PREPARATION TIME: 20 minutes (plus 20 minutes cooking time)

This works as a main dish—just serve over the rice you made while the vegetables simmered.

1	tablespoon vegetable oil
1	small onion, chopped
3	cloves garlic, minced
1/4	teaspoon cayenne
1/2	teaspoon ground cumin
1	tablespoon ground coriander
2	teaspoons ground cardamom
1/2	teaspoon turmeric
1/2	teaspoon cinnamon
1 1/2	teaspoons fresh ginger, grated
1/4	teaspoon salt
2	cups cauliflower florets
2	carrots, sliced
2	zucchinis, sliced
1/2	pound fresh green beans, trimmed and cut into 1-inch pieces
2	cups vegetable broth
	Cooked rice

Heat a pot with the oil over medium heat. Add the onion and cook until soft, about 5 minutes. Add garlic and the next 8 ingredients and stir constantly for about 1 minute, being careful not to burn the garlic. Add the vegetables and stir well to mix. Add to the broth, cover, reduce heat, and simmer about 20 minutes until the vegetables are tender. Serve over the rice.

Serves 4

Each serving provides:

131	Calories	21 g	Carbohydrate
5 g	Protein	162 mg	Sodium
4 g	Fat	0 mg	Cholesterol

Pepper and Bean Enchiladas with Green Sauce

PREPARATION TIME: 35 minutes (plus 15 minutes baking time, includes making the sauce)

Enchiladas with this green sauce are a snap to make, and a filling dinner.

	Mexican Green Sauce (see page 26)
2	tablespoons vegetable oil
2	teaspoons ground cumin
1	tablespoon ground coriander
1	sweet red pepper, julienned
2	cups black beans, canned okay (see Introduction, page 3)
16	fresh corn tortillas
1	small onion, chopped
1/2	cup Cheddar cheese (optional)

While the sauce is cooking, add the oil to a separate saucepan and stir in cumin and coriander. Add the pepper and sauté for about 5 minutes. Add beans to the pan, mix well, and cook until warm.

Pour the finished sauce onto a plate and dip the tortillas in the sauce. Spoon 2 tablespoons of bean-pepper mixture along with a teaspoon of the onion into the tortillas. Add cheese if desired. Fold over and pin with a toothpick. Repeat, placing all of the tortillas in baking dishes. Pour remaining sauce over and bake until bubbly, about 15 minutes.

Serves 6 to 8

Each serving not including sauce provides:

230	Calories	39 g	Carbohydrate
7 g	Protein	340 mg	Sodium
5 g	Fat	0 mg	Cholesterol

Spicy Spinach Enchiladas

PREPARATION TIME: 30 minutes (plus 10 minutes baking time)

Here is a lower fat alternative to the traditional cheese enchilada, often the only kind available to those who don't eat meat.

1	tablespoon olive oil
1/2	small onion, chopped
1/4	pound mushrooms, sliced
10	ounces spinach, stemmed
3	teaspoons vegetable oil
6	corn tortillas
	Spicy Enchilada Sauce (page 28)
1	cup grated Cheddar or Monterey Jack cheese

Preheat oven to 350°. Heat the olive oil in a skillet and add the onion. Sauté for 4 minutes, then add the mushrooms and cook another 3 minutes. Place the spinach on top and, stirring constantly, cook until spinach wilts and is cooked throughout, about 3 minutes. Remove from heat. Heat 1 teaspoon of the vegetable oil in a skillet and cook a tortilla on both sides, until warm but not crisp. Repeat with another tortilla, then repeat with the remaining oil and tortillas. Place about 3/4 cup of the sauce to cover the bottom of a baking dish. Put about 1/3 cup of the spinach mixture into each tortilla and place in the dish in a row. Pour another 1 1/2 cups, or more, of the sauce over the tortillas and top with cheese. Bake for 10 minutes.

Makes 6 enchiladas, serves 3 to 4

Each serving provides:

404	Calories	37 g	Carbohydrate
14 g	Protein	523 mg	Sodium
24 g	Fat	29 mg	Cholesterol

Grilled Vegetables with Ginger Barbecue Sauce

PREPARATION TIME: 30 minutes (plus 25 minutes simmer time)

The non-vegetarians in your house will want to try this barbecue sauce with meat. It's also great with vegetables and matches perfectly the smoky flavor of summer barbecue.

2	medium onions, chopped
2	tablespoons vegetable oil
5	cloves garlic, chopped
1	2-inch piece ginger, sliced
2	cups tomato sauce
2	tablespoons Dijon mustard
1/3	cup vinegar
1	cup water
1	bay leaf
1/4	cup Worcestershire sauce
2	tablespoons brown sugar
2	tablespoons molasses
1/2	teaspoon cayenne
1/4	teaspoon salt
3	eggplants, peeled, sliced, and grilled 6 to 7 minutes per side
3	sweet peppers, peeled, seeded, sliced into thick strips, brushed with olive oil, and grilled until just blackened, about 4 minutes per side
2	zucchinis, sliced, grilled about 4 minutes per side Cooked rice

Sauté the onion in the oil for 3 to 4 minutes, then add garlic and sauté until soft, another 3 minutes. Place in a blender or food processor with the ginger and puree. Return to the skillet with the remaining ingredients except grilled vegetables and rice, and bring to a boil. Reduce heat and simmer about 25 minutes, stirring occasionally. Place vegetables on rice and pour sauce on top.

Serves 4

Each serving not including rice provides:

357	Calories	67 g	Carbohydrate
8 g	Protein	1250 mg	Sodium
10 g	Fat	0 mg	Cholesterol

Zucchini Stuffed with Herbs and Cheese

PREPARATION TIME: 25 minutes (plus 25 minutes baking time)

These stuffed zucchinis go nicely with a green salad, which can be fixed while this bakes.

6	medium zucchinis, whole
3	cloves garlic, minced
1	cup mushrooms, chopped
1/2	teaspoon fresh dill or 1/4 teaspoon dried
1/2	teaspoon fresh thyme or 1/4 teaspoon dried
1/2	teaspoon fresh marjoram or 1/4 teaspoon dried
2	tablespoons olive oil
2/3	cup white wine
1	cup bread crumbs
1 1/4	cups Parmesan cheese, grated

Preheat oven to 350°. Steam the zucchinis whole for 5 minutes, until just softening. Trim the ends and cut in half lengthwise. Scoop out the center, making a hollow for the stuffing.

Sauté the garlic, mushrooms, and herbs in the oil over medium-low heat for about 10 minutes. Add the white wine, increase heat to high, and cook 4 minutes or until the wine is reduced by half. Remove the mushroom mixture to a separate bowl and combine with the bread crumbs and 1/4 cup of the Parmesan. Place the mixture into the zucchini halves and top with the remaining Parmesan. Bake in an oiled baking dish for 25 minutes, until brown.

Serves 4

Each serving provides:

329	Calories	27 g	Carbohydrate
16 g	Protein	659 mg	Sodium
16 g	Fat	21 mg	Cholesterol

Four-Alarm Stir-Fry

Preparation Time: 25 minutes

This stir-fry is for those who enjoy very hot foods. The key is to keep stirring—have everything chopped or grated and ready to add before you begin. As with most stir-fries, this is a complete meal all by itself.

1	teaspoon cornstarch dissolved in $1/4$ cup vegetable broth or water
1	tablespoon soy sauce
1	teaspoon sesame oil
$1/2$	teaspoon crushed red pepper flakes
2	teaspoons honey
3	tablespoons vegetable oil
2	carrots, peeled and sliced
10	mushrooms, quartered
1	sweet onion, cut in half and thinly sliced
1	clove garlic, minced
1	inch fresh ginger, grated or minced
1	sweet red or green pepper, diced
2	tablespoons jalapeño, seeded and finely chopped
	Cooked rice

Combine the cornstarch and broth with the soy sauce, sesame oil, red pepper flakes, and honey to make the sauce. In a skillet or wok, heat the oil over high heat and add the carrots and mushrooms, stirring constantly for about 5 minutes. Add onion and stir another minute, then garlic and ginger and stir another minute, being careful not to let the garlic burn. Add peppers and cook another 2 minutes. Pour in sauce and bring to a boil, stirring constantly. Remove from heat and spoon over rice.

Serves 4

Each serving not including rice provides:

168	Calories	15 g	Carbohydrate
2 g	Protein	280 mg	Sodium
12 g	Fat	0 mg	Cholesterol

Black Bean and Jicama Tostadas

PREPARATION TIME: 20 minutes (includes making salsa)

This delicious salsa practically makes a meal in itself. If you choose, you can opt to top with cheese, sour cream, or even tomato salsa.

	Black Bean Salsa (see page 18)
1/4	cup vegetable oil
6	corn tortillas
	Monterey Jack or Cheddar cheese, grated (optional)
	Sour cream (optional)

Make the salsa as directed. Mix well. In a skillet, heat the vegetable oil until hot, then add the tortillas one at a time. Fry the tortillas, turning once, until crisp, up to a minute on each side. Drain on paper towels, top with the salsa or topping of your choice, and serve.

Makes 6 tostadas

Each tostada provides:

234	Calories	29 g	Carbohydrate
7 g	Protein	402 mg	Sodium
10 g	Fat	0 mg	Cholesterol

Pineapple Stir-Fried Rice

PREPARATION TIME: 25 minutes

Cold rice is the key to successful stir-fried rice. This is perfect for leftover rice, or make rice in the morning and leave it in the refrigerator all day so it will be ready to stir-fry when you get home.

2	tablespoons sesame or peanut oil
1	3-inch piece fresh ginger, grated
1	jalapeño, seeded and minced
1	clove garlic, minced
1/4	cup lemon zest
3	cups cooked cold rice
1	cup pineapple, finely chopped
1	cup fresh cilantro, finely chopped

Heat a skillet or wok over medium-high heat then add the oil, ginger, pepper, and garlic and stir-fry 1 minute, being careful not to burn the ginger or garlic. Add the lemon zest and rice and stir until heated. Stir in the pineapple and cilantro until heated.

Serves 4

Each serving provides:

307	Calories	55 g	Carbohydrate
5 g	Protein	7 mg	Sodium
7 g	Fat	0 mg	Cholesterol

Fruit Curry over Rice

PREPARATION TIME: 30 minutes

This sweet dish makes a delightful dinner. I use frozen fruit which makes it quick and easy as well. Feel free to substitute fruit you have on hand, such as grapes or pears. Serve a vegetable or cucumber salad on the side.

2	tablespoons olive oil
1/8	teaspoon cayenne
1/4	teaspoon ground cumin
1	teaspoon *each* ground cardamom and coriander
1/2	teaspoon turmeric
1	teaspon paprika
1/4	teaspoon cinnamon
1/8	teaspoon salt
1 1/2	tablespoons fresh ginger, grated
5	tablespoons vegetable broth
1	cup fresh or frozen peaches, peeled and chopped
1	cup fresh or frozen plums, peeled and chopped
1/4	cup pineapple, minced
2	tablespoons brown sugar
	Cooked rice

Heat the oil over low heat and add spices. Stir for 3 to 4 minutes, add vegetable broth, and increase heat to a boil. Reduce broth by about a third, then add fruit and brown sugar. Cook until syrupy, about 20 minutes. Pour over rice (or over grilled vegetables).

Serves 4

Each serving not including rice provides:

158	Calories	24 g	Carbohydrate
1 g	Protein	72 mg	Sodium
8 g	Fat	0 mg	Cholesterol

Baked Zucchini with Pepper Sauce

PREPARATION TIME: 25 minutes

I use roasted red peppers from jars when I'm in a hurry, although they don't offer the flavor of freshly roasted peppers. To roast your own, see page 4. A good dish with rice.

1	tablespoon jalapeño, seeded and minced
1/2	teaspoon dried oregano
1/8	teaspoon salt
1/4	teaspoon pepper
2	tablespoons olive oil
4	roasted red peppers, seeded and chopped
6	zucchinis
	Parmesan cheese (optional)

Preheat oven to 375°. Sauté the jalapeño, oregano, salt, and pepper in olive oil for 3 to 4 minutes, then remove to a blender or food processor, add the roasted peppers, and puree. Blanch the zucchini in boiling water for about 3 minutes.

Remove and rinse under cold water. Trim and cut each zucchini lengthwise, then scoop out seeds. Place zucchini in an oiled baking dish, rub with a little olive oil, and bake 6 minutes. Spoon sauce into zucchini and bake another 12 minutes. Top with Parmesan, if desired, for the last 2 to 3 minutes of baking time.

Serves 4

Each serving provides:

108	Calories	11 g	Carbohydrate
3 g	Protein	74 mg	Sodium
7 g	Fat	0 mg	Cholesterol

Vegetables in Raw Tomato Sauce

PREPARATION TIME: 30 minutes (plus standing time—recommended for best flavor—of 90 minutes)

This Provençal sauce is traditionally served with fish but I find the style goes well with sautéed and raw vegetables. With all these fresh ingredients I like to use fresh herbs, although dried thyme does pretty well. Top with a little cheese if you like.

1/4	cup extra-virgin olive oil
8	medium, ripe tomatoes, peeled, seeded, and chopped
1	tablespoon red wine vinegar
5	niçoise or calamata olives, pitted and finely chopped
3	cloves garlic, finely chopped or minced
1/8	teaspoon salt
1/4	teaspoon pepper
3	carrots, trimmed and sliced
2	medium zucchinis, trimmed and sliced
1	head broccoli florets, chopped
1	tablespoon fresh parsley, chopped
2	teaspoons fresh rosemary, chopped
2	teaspoons fresh thyme, chopped, or 1 teaspoon dried
2	teaspoons chives or scallions, chopped

Combine one half of the oil, the tomatoes, vinegar, olives, garlic, salt, and pepper in a bowl and let sit for 90 minutes or more for flavors to blend. Briefly steam the carrots to soften slightly, about 3 minutes. Heat the remaining oil in a skillet and add the carrots, zucchini, and broccoli. Cook until just crisp-tender, about 7 to 10 minutes. Stir the herbs into the sauce. Serve the vegetables with the tomato sauce spooned on top.

Serves 4

Each serving provides:

226	Calories	22 g	Carbohydrate
6 g	Protein	156 mg	Sodium
15 g	Fat	0 mg	Cholesterol

Vegetables in Spanish Rice

PREPARATION TIME: 40 minutes (plus 20 minutes cooking time)

This dish takes a little longer to prepare, but it's worth it. It's a complete meal with vegetables, starches—and a little spice.

3	cloves garlic, minced
1	onion, minced
1	sweet pepper, seeded and diced
3	tablespoons extra-virgin olive oil
1/2	teaspoon cayenne
1/8	teaspoon salt
1/4	teaspoon pepper
1/2	pound red or Yukon gold potatoes, diced
1/2	cup canned tomatoes, drained
5	cups vegetable broth or water
1	pound fresh green beans, trimmed and cut into 1-inch pieces
1	16-ounce can red kidney beans, drained
1	pound fresh asparagus, cut into 1-inch pieces
1	pound fresh peas, thawed if frozen
2	cups rice

In a large pot, sauté the garlic, onion, and pepper in the oil until soft, about 10 minutes. Add spices, potatoes, and tomatoes and continue to sauté for another 10 minutes. Add the broth and bring to a boil, then add beans. Reduce heat, cover, and cook for 5 minutes, then add remaining ingredients, return to a boil, reduce heat, and cover, cooking 20 to 25 more minutes, or until rice is done.

Serves 6

Each serving provides:

517	Calories	97 g	Carbohydrate
16 g	Protein	268 mg	Sodium
8 g	Fat	0 mg	Cholesterol

Sweet & Sour Cabbage

PREPARATION TIME: 25 minutes

The cabbage really soaks up the sweet & sour flavors.

1	small onion, cut in half and thinly sliced
2	carrots, thinly sliced
1	tablespoon peanut oil
1/2	head green cabbage, chopped
1/3	cup honey
1/3	cup cider vinegar
1	teaspoon fresh ginger, grated
2	teaspoons cornstarch
1	teaspoon soy sauce
	Cooked rice

Sauté the onion and carrot in the oil over medium-high heat, stirring to keep the onion from burning. Add cabbage and continue cooking for 3 minutes. Add 1/4 cup of water, cover, reduce heat, and cook for 10 minutes. Combine remaining ingredients, except the rice, stirring the cornstarch to dissolve. Add to the vegetables and stir until sauce thickens. Serve over rice.

Serves 4

Each serving provides:

184	Calories	39 g	Carbohydrate
3 g	Protein	121 mg	Sodium
4 g	Fat	0 mg	Cholesterol

Index

A

Andrew's mushroom ta-rito, 200
Apple coleslaw, curried, 56
Asian "pesto" pasta, 169
Asparagus
  with ginger-lemon dressing, 95
  and leek pasta, 160–161
Avocado salsa, spicy, 22
Avocado soup, 91

B

Baked zucchini with pepper sauce,
  222–223
Balsamic vinegar, 2
Basil and parmesan ravioli, 140–141
Basil-cilantro pesto, 69
Bean salad
  black bean, 62
  new Mexican, 59
  with orange vinaigrette, 68
Beans
  cooking, 3–4
  in salads, 34
Black bean and jicama tostadas, 218
Black bean and pepper salad, 43
Black bean one-skillet casserole, 196
Black bean salsa, 18–19, 218
Black bean vegetable salad, 62
Black beans
  in bean salad with orange vinai-
    grette, 68
  in colorful couscous casserole,
    198–199
  in colorful rice and black bean
    salad, 60–61
  in gingered black beans, 112
  in pepper and bean enchiladas
    with green sauce, 208–209
  in spicy black bean and pasta
    salad, 38–39
  in spicy greens and beans, 104
  in three-pepper chili, 184–185
  using canned, 3

using dried, 3
in vegetarian burritos, 182–183
Bleu cheese and roasted pecan
  salad, 54
Bow-tie pasta with mint, 145
Burritos, vegetarian, 182–183

C

Cabbage soup, 79
Cabbage, sweet and sour, 228
Caramelized shallot, mushroom, and
  fennel quesadillas, 190–191
Carrot and cilantro rice, 115
Carrots
  and green beans, saucy, 123
  sweet and hot, 107
Casseroles
  black bean one-skillet, 196
  colorful couscous, 198–199
  fiery zucchini, 194
  vegetable-pepper, 195
Cayenne pepper, uses of. *See* Pep-
  pers, hot
Chile pepper and sour cream que-
  sadillas, 178–179
Chili powder, 4
Chili, three-pepper, 184–185
Chutney, Virginia's mango, 30–31
Cilantro (coriander), fresh versus
  dried, 3
Cold, spicy cucumber soup, 90
Cold tomato and roasted pepper
  soup, 88
Cold-pressed oils, 2
Coleslaw
  curried apple, 56
  jicama slaw with cilantro vinai-
    grette, 58
  sweet and spicy, 42
Colorful couscous casserole,
  198–199
Colorful rice and black bean salad,
  60–61

Companion dishes, 93
  asparagus with ginger-lemon
    dressing, 95
  carrot and cilantro rice, 115
  curried fried rice, 129
  gingered black beans, 112
  green beans in hazelnut butter, 124
  grilled ginger-lemon
    vegetables, 121
  gruyere potatoes, 102
  hot, spicy rice and raisins, 96–97
  JoAnn's potatoes with chaat
    masala, 108
  lemon herb rice, 120
  Mediterranean rice, 110
  pineapple-curry rice, 125
  quick Mexican vegetables, 103
  quick spinach with feta, 111
  raw vegetables with soy-ginger
    sauce, 128
  rice with cheese, 106
  rice with fruit, 101
  roasted cabbage with peanut
    sauce, 126–127
  simple and spicy zucchini
    fritters, 113
  simple summer vegetables, 98
  snappy garbanzos, 109
  snow peas and red peppers, 99
  Spanish rice, 114
  spicy carrots and green
    beans, 123
  spicy green beans, 105
  spicy greens and beans, 104
  spicy potato pancakes, 122
  stir-fried red potatoes, 94
  sweet and hot carrots, 107
  tamarind rice, 116
  teriyaki mushrooms and
    peppers, 117
  Thai vegetable curry, 130–131
  tomatoes with parsley, 100
  vegetables with ginger-sesame
    sauce, 118–119
Corn chowder, spicy, 84–85
Corn salad, spicy, 65
Corn soup, curried, 78
Creamy gazpacho, 87
Cucumber and dill salad, 63

Cucumber salad, Thai, 55
Cucumber-dill dressing, 12
Cumin and dill dressing, 12–13
Curried corn soup, 78
Curried fried rice, 129
Curried vegetable soup, 75
Curried vegetables, 206–207
Curried Waldorf salad, 40
Curry powder, 4

D
Dilled zucchini soup, 74
Dressings, 9
  cilantro vinaigrette, 58
  cucumber-dill, 12
  cumin and dill, 12–13
  ginger-lemon, 95
  Greek, 14–15
  hot vinegar, 14
  jalapeño and lime, 11
  orange vinaigrette, 68
  three fresh (rosemary vinaigrette,
    honey mustard, and wine
    vinaigrette), 16–17

E
Enchilada sauce, spicy, 28–29,
  210–211
Enchiladas
  pepper and bean, with green
    sauce, 208–209
  spicy spinach, 210–211

F
Farmer's market, 93
Fennel, caramelized, 146–147
Fettuccine
  fresh tomato, 168
  with garlic and zucchini, 148
  with peas and peppers, 149
Fiery zucchini casserole, 194
Focaccia used in pizza,
  142–143, 155
Four-alarm stir-fry, 216–217
French Paradox, 5
Fresh tomato fettuccine, 168
Frittata, Mex-Italian, 197
Fruit curry over rice, 220–221

G

Garlic, selecting fresh, 3
Gazpacho, 87
Ginger
health benefits of, 154
using fresh, 2
Ginger barbecue sauce, 212–213
Ginger, daikon, and sweet pepper
tostadas, 202–203
Ginger-lime pasta salad with
vegetables, 36
Gingered black beans, 112
Greek dressing, 14–15
Green bean salad, 57
Green beans in hazelnut
butter, 124
Green sauce, Mexican, 26, 197,
208–209
Grilled ginger-lemon vegetables, 121
Grilled vegetables with ginger barbe-
cue sauce, 212–213
Gruyere potatoes, 102

H

Harissa sauce, 18
Hazelnut, mascarpone, and
gorgonzola ravioli,
172–173
Herbs
fresh versus dried, 2–3
storing fresh, 3
ways to use fresh, table of, 7
Honey mustard dressing, 17
Hot and spicy fried rice, 201
Hot pepper oil, 158
Hot pesto sauce, 28
Hot, spicy rice and raisins, 96–97
Hot vinegar for soups or dressings,
14, 80–81

J

Jalapeño and lime dressing, 11
Jalapeño peppers, uses of.
See Peppers, hot
Jalapeño spread, 20
Jicama
in black bean and jicama
tostadas, 218

in jicama slaw with cilantro
vinaigrette, 58
in potato-jicama salad, 52–53
texture and flavor of, 44
JoAnn's potatoes with chaat
masala, 108

L

Lasagna sheets, purchasing, 133
Lemon herb rice, 120
Lemon spaghetti, 138
Lime-curry orzo, 136–137
Linguine with lemon and
caramelized fennel, 146–147

M

Main dishes, 175
Andrew's mushroom ta-rito, 200
baked zucchini with pepper sauce,
222–223
black bean and jicama tostadas, 218
black bean one-skillet
casserole, 196
caramelized shallot, mushroom,
and fennel quesadillas, 190–191
chile pepper and sour cream
quesadillas, 178–179
colorful couscous casserole,
198–199
curried vegetables, 206–207
fiery zucchini casserole, 194
four-alarm stir-fry, 216–217
fruit curry over rice, 220–221
ginger, daikon, and sweet pepper
tostadas, 202–203
grilled vegetables with ginger barbecue sauce, 212–213
hot and spicy fried rice, 201
Mexican "quiche," 204–205
Mexican stuffed peppers, 192–193
Mex-Italian frittata, 197
mushroom and cilantro tostadas,
188–189
pepper and bean enchiladas with
green sauce, 208–209
pineapple stir-fried rice, 219
spicy shish kabobs, 186–187
spicy spinach enchiladas,
210–211

Main dishes, *continued*
  sweet and sour and spicy,
    180–181
  sweet and sour cabbage, 228
  three-pepper chili, 184–185
  vegetable stir-fry with ginger
    sauce, 176–177
  vegetable-pepper casserole, 195
  vegetables in raw tomato sauce,
    224–225
  vegetables in Spanish rice,
    226–227
  vegetarian burritos, 182–183
  zucchini stuffed with herbs and
    cheese, 214–215
Mango chutney, Virginia's, 30–31
Mediterranean rice, 110
Mexican green sauce, 26, 197,
  208–209
Mexican "quiche," 204–205
Mexican stuffed peppers,
  192–193
Mex-Italian frittata, 197
Mint, bow-tie pasta with, 145
Mushroom and cilantro tostadas,
  188–189
Mushroom-ginger pasta, 154

N
New Mexican bean salad, 59

O
Oils, tips for using, 2
Olive oil, extra-virgin, 2

P
Pasta, 133–134
  in Asian "pesto" pasta, 169
  in asparagus and leek pasta,
    160–161
  in basil and parmesan ravioli,
    140–141
  in bow-tie pasta with
    mint, 145
  in fettuccine with garlic and zuc-
    chini, 148
  in fettuccine with peas and pep-
    pers, 149
  in fresh tomato fettuccine, 168

  in ginger-lime pasta salad with
    vegetables, 36–37
  in hazelnut, mascarpone, and gor-
    gonzola ravioli, 172–173
  in lemon spaghetti, 138
  in lime-curry orzo, 136–137
  in linguine with lemon and
    caramelized fennel, 146–147
  in mushroom-ginger pasta, 154
  in penne with broccoli, 159
  in penne with calamata
    olives, 139
  in penne with peppers, 144
  in penne with walnuts and basil,
    166–167
  in peppers stuffed with pasta and
    cheese, 152–153
  in quick lemon-ricotta ravioli,
    150–151
  in roasted tomato and raw veg-
    etable, 156–157
  in spaghetti verdura, 164
  in spaghetti with hot pepper
    sauce, 158
  in spicy black bean and pasta
    salad, 38–39
  in spicy gemelli with radicchio,
    olives, and tomato, 165
  in spicy pasta and chickpea salad,
    66–67
  in summer pasta, 135
  in sweet pepper cannelloni,
    170–171
  in Thai noodle salad, 46–47
  in warm pasta salad, 45
  in ziti vegetable salad, 64
  in ziti with herbs, 162–163
Peach salsa, spicy, 23
Peeling and seeding tomatoes, 4
Penne
  with broccoli, 159
  with calamata olives, 139
  with peppers, 144
  with walnuts and basil,
    166–167
Pepper and bean enchiladas with
  green sauce, 208–209
Pepper sauce, 222–223
Pepperpot soup, 72–73

Peppers, hot, 3
   in companion dishes, 96–97, 99,
      105–108, 112, 114, 115,
      125–127
   in dressings, 11, 14
   in harissa, 18
   in main dishes, 178–207,
      212–213, 216–217, 219–223,
      226–227
   in pasta dishes, 134, 135–137,
      146–147, 155–158, 162–163,
      166–169
   roasting, 4
   in salads, 35, 46, 60–61,
      62, 65
   in salsas, 19, 23
   in sauces, 21, 29
   in soups, 72–73, 75, 76, 78, 83,
      86–89
   in spread, 20
   in stew, 82
Peppers stuffed with pasta and
      cheese, 152–153
Peppers, table of uses for, 8
Pesto sauce
   in Asian "pesto" pasta, 169
   basil-cilantro, 69
   hot, 28
Pineapple salsa, 24
Pineapple stir-fried rice, 219
Pineapple-curry rice, 125
Pizza
   ratatouille, 142–143
   Sicilian, 155
Pizza sauce, 27, 134
Potato-jicama salad, 52–53
Potatoes
   gruyere, 102
   JoAnn's, with chaat masala, 108
   stir-fried red, 94
Protein for vegetarians, 5

Q
Quesadillas
   caramelized shallot, mushroom,
      and fennel, 190–191
   chile pepper and sour cream,
      178–179
"Quiche," Mexican, 204–205

Quick lemon-ricotta ravioli,
      150–151
Quick Mexican vegetables, 103,
      204–205
Quick spinach with feta, 111
Quick vegetable stew, 82

R
Ratatouille pizza, 142–143
Ravioli dough or wonton
      wrappers, 133
   in basil and parmesan ravioli,
      140–141
   in hazelnut, mascarpone, and gor-
      gonzola ravioli, 172–173
   in quick lemon-ricotta ravioli,
      150–151
Raw tomato sauce, 224–225
Raw vegetables with soy-ginger
      sauce, 128
Red pepper soup, 83
Rice dishes
   baked zucchini with pepper sauce,
      222–223
   caramelized shallot, mushroom,
      and fennel quesadillas, 190–191
   carrot and cilantro rice, 115
   curried fried rice, 129
   curried vegetables, 206–207
   four-alarm stir-fry, 216–217
   fruit curry over rice, 220–221
   grilled vegetables with ginger bar-
      becue sauce, 212–213
   hot and spicy fried rice, 201
   hot, spicy rice and raisins, 96–97
   lemon herb rice, 120
   Mediterranean rice, 110
   Mexican stuffed peppers,
      192–193
   pineapple stir-fried rice, 219
   pineapple-curry rice, 125
   rice with cheese, 106
   rice with fruit, 101
   Spanish rice, 114
   sweet and sour and spicy,
      180–181
   tamarind rice, 116
   vegetable stir-fry with ginger
      sauce, 176–177

Rice dishes, *continued*
  vegetable-pepper casserole, 195
  vegetables in Spanish rice,
    226–227
Rice vinegar, 2
Roasted cabbage with peanut sauce,
  126–127
Roasted tomato
  and habanero sauce, 21
  and raw vegetable pasta, 156–157
Roasting hot or sweet peppers, 4
Rosemary vinaigrette dressing, 16

S

Salads, 33–34
  bean salad with orange vinai-
    grette, 68
  black bean and pepper, 43
  black bean vegetable, 62
  bleu cheese and roasted
    pecan, 54
  colorful rice and black bean,
    60–61
  cucumber and dill, 63
  curried apple coleslaw, 56
    curried Waldorf, 40
  ginger-lime pasta salad with
    vegetables, 36–37
  green bean, 57
  jicama slaw with cilantro vinai-
    grette, 58
  new Mexican bean, 59
  potato-jicama, 52–53
  spicy black bean and pasta, 34,
    38–39
  spicy corn, 65
  spicy pasta and chickpea, 66–67
  spicy vegetable, 35
  sweet and spicy slaw, 42
  sweet spinach, 41
  Thai cucumber, 55
  Thai noodle, 46–47
  vegetable, 44
  warm pasta, 45
  watercress, gorgonzola, and pear,
    50–51
  ziti vegetable, 64
  zucchini, tomato, tarragon and
    white wine, 48–49

Salsas, 9–10
  black bean, 18–19, 218
  pineapple, 24
  spicy avocado, 22
  spicy peach, 23
Sauces, 9–10
  ginger, 176–177
  ginger barbecue, 212–213
  ginger-sesame, 118–119
  harissa, 18
  hot pepper, 158
  hot pesto, 28
  Mexican green, 26, 197, 208–209
  peanut, 126–127
  pepper, 222–223
  pizza, 27, 134
  raw tomato, 224–225
  roasted tomato and habanero, 21
  soy-ginger, 128
  spicy enchilada, 28–29, 210–211
  very fast tomato, 25, 135,
    170–171
  Virginia's mango chutney, 30–31
Saucy carrots and green beans, 123
Serrano peppers, uses of. *See*
  Peppers, hot
Shish kabobs, spicy, 188–189
Sicilian pizza, 155
Side dishes. *See* Companion dishes
Simple and spicy zucchini
  fritters, 113
Simple summer vegetables, 98
Snappy garbanzos, 109
Snow peas and red peppers, 99
Soups, 69
  avocado, 91
  cabbage, 79
  cold, spicy cucumber, 90
  cold tomato and roasted
    pepper, 88
  curried corn, 78
  curried vegetable, 75
  dilled zucchini, 74
  gazpacho and creamy
    gazpacho, 87
  pepperpot, 72–73
  red pepper, 83
  spicy corn chowder, 84–85
  spicy tomato, 86

Thai, 76–77
tomato, pepper, and cilantro, 89
vegetable broth, 70–71
zucchini-basil, 80–81
Spaghetti
with hot pepper sauce, 158
verdura, 164
Spanish rice, 114
Spices, using fresh, 2–3
Spicy avocado salsa, 22
Spicy black bean and pasta salad,
38–39
Spicy corn chowder, 84–85
Spicy corn salad, 65
Spicy enchilada sauce, 28–29,
210–211
Spicy gemelli with radicchio, olives,
and tomato, 165
Spicy green beans, 105
Spicy greens and beans, 104
Spicy pasta and chickpea salad,
66–67
Spicy peach salsa, 23
Spicy potato pancakes, 122
Spicy shish kabobs, 186–187
Spicy spinach enchiladas, 210–211
Spicy tomato soup, 86
Spicy vegetable salad, 35
Spinach salad, sweet, 41
Spread, jalapeño, 20
Stew, quick vegetable, 82
Stir-fry
four-alarm, 216–217
with ginger sauce, 176–177
pineapple, 219
red potatoes, 94
Summer pasta, 135
Sweet and hot carrots, 107
Sweet and sour and spicy, 180–181
Sweet and sour cabbage, 228
Sweet and spicy slaw, 42
Sweet pepper cannelloni, 170–171
Sweet spinach salad, 41

T
Tamarind rice, 116
Teriyaki mushrooms and peppers,
117
Thai cucumber salad, 55

Thai noodle salad, 46–47
Thai soup, 76–77
Thai vegetable curry, 130–131
Three-pepper chili, 184–185
Tomato, pepper, and cilantro
soup, 89
Tomato sauce
raw, 224–225
very fast, 25, 135
Tomato soup, spicy, 86
Tomatoes
peeling and seeding, 4
roasting, 156
Tomatoes with parsley, 100
Tostadas
black bean and jicama, 218
ginger, daikon, and sweet pepper,
202–203
mushroom and cilantro,
188–189

V
Vegetable broth, 70–71
in companion dishes, 114, 115,
116, 118–119, 120, 129,
130–131
in main dishes, 186–187,
192–193, 195, 196, 206–207,
216–217, 220–221, 226–227
in salads, 38, 60–61
in sauces, 29
in soups, 72–73, 74, 75, 76–77,
78, 79, 83, 84–85, 90, 91
Vegetable curry, Thai, 130–131
Vegetable salad, 44
black bean, 62
ziti, 64
Vegetable soup
basil-cilantro pesto added to, 69
curried, 75
Vegetable stew, quick, 82
Vegetable stir-fry with ginger sauce,
176–177
Vegetable-pepper casserole, 195
Vegetables
curried, 206–207
with ginger-sesame sauce,
118–119
grilled ginger-lemon, 121

Vegetables, *continued*
　grilled, with ginger barbecue
　　sauce, 212–213
　quick Mexican, 103, 204–205
　in raw tomato sauce, 224–225
　raw, with soy-ginger sauce, 128
　simple summer, 98
　in Spanish rice, 226–227
　vitamins in, 6
Vegetarian burritos, 182–183
Vegetarians, 1, 5–6, 175
Very fast tomato sauce, 25, 135,
　170–171
Vinegar
　balsamic, 2
　hot, 14, 80–81
　wine, 2
Virginia's mango chutney, 30–31

W
Waldorf salad, curried, 40
Warm pasta salad, 45

Watercress, gorgonzola, and pear
　salad, 50–51
Wine, health value of, 5
Wine vinaigrette dressing, 17
Wonton wrappers to make ravioli,
　133, 140–141, 150–151,
　172–173

Z
Ziti
　with herbs, 162–163
　vegetable salad, 64
Zucchini, baked, with pepper sauce,
　222–223
Zucchini casserole, fiery, 194
Zucchini fritters, simple and spicy, 113
Zucchini soup, dilled, 74
Zucchini stuffed with herbs and
　cheese, 214–215
Zucchini, tomato, tarragon and white
　wine salad, 48–49
Zucchini-basil soup, 80–81

International Conversion Chart

These are not exact equivalents: they have been slightly rounded to make measuring easier.

Liquid Measurements

American	Imperial	Metric	Australian
2 tablespoons (1 oz.)	1 fl. oz.	30 ml	1 tablespoon
1/4 cup (2 oz.)	2 fl. oz.	60 ml	2 tablespoons
1/3 cup (3 oz.)	3 fl. oz.	80 ml	1/4 cup
1/2 cup (4 oz.)	4 fl. oz.	125 ml	1/3 cup
2/3 cup (5 oz.)	5 fl. oz.	165 ml	1/2 cup
3/4 cup (6 oz.)	6 fl. oz.	185 ml	2/3 cup
1 cup (8 oz.)	8 fl. oz.	250 ml	3/4 cup

Spoon Measurements

American	Metric
1/4 teaspoon	1 ml
1/2 teaspoon	2 ml
1 teaspoon	5 ml
1 tablespoon	15 ml

Weights

US/UK	Metric
1 oz.	30 grams (g)
2 oz.	60 g
4 oz. (1/4 lb)	125 g
5 oz. (1/3 lb)	155 g
6 oz.	185 g
7 oz.	220 g
8 oz. (1/2 lb)	250 g
10 oz.	315 g
12 oz. (3/4 lb)	375 g
14 oz.	440 g
16 oz. (1 lb)	500 g
2 lbs	1 kg

Oven Temperatures

Farenheit	Centigrade	Gas
250	120	1/2
300	150	2
325	160	3
350	180	4
375	190	5
400	200	6
450	230	8

To Order Books

Please send me the following items:

Quantity	Title	Unit Price	Total
_____	**101 Meatless Family Dishes**	$ 14.95	$ _____
_____	**101 Great Sauces**	$ 9.95	$ _____
_____	**Cooking with Herbs**	$ 14.95	$ _____
_____	_____	$ _____	$ _____
_____	_____	$ _____	$ _____

*Shipping and Handling depend on Subtotal.

Subtotal	Shipping/Handling
$0.00–$14.99	$3.00
$15.00–$29.99	$4.00
$30.00–$49.99	$6.00
$50.00–$99.99	$10.00
$100.00–$199.99	$13.50
$200.00+	Call for Quote

Foreign and all Priority Request orders:
Call Order Entry department
for price quote at 916-632-4400

This chart represents the total retail price of books only (before applicable discounts are taken).

Subtotal	$ _____
Deduct 10% when ordering 3–5 books	$ _____
7.25% Sales Tax (CA only)	$ _____
8.25% Sales Tax (TN only)	$ _____
5% Sales Tax (MD and IN only)	$ _____
7% GST Tax (Canada Only)	$ _____
Shipping and Handling*	$ _____
Total Order	$ _____

By Telephone: With MC, Visa, or American Express, call 800-632-8676 or 916-632-4400
Mon–Fri, 8:30–4:30

WWW: http://www.primapublishing.com

By Internet E-mail: sales@primapub.com

By Mail: Just fill out the information below and send with your remittance to:

**Prima Publishing
P.O. Box 1260BK
Rocklin, CA 95677**

Name _____

Address_____

City _____ State _____ ZIP_____

MC/Visa/American Express# _____ Exp. _____

Check/money order enclosed for $_____ Payable to Prima Publishing

Daytime telephone _____

Signature _____